INSTRUCTOR'S GUIDE TO ACCOMPANY

T5-DHI-376

TODAY'S TECHNICIAN™

Manual Transmissions and Transaxles

Fourth Edition

Jack Erjavec

Don Knowles

THOMSON

DELMAR LEARNING™   Australia   Canada   Mexico   Singapore   Spain   United Kingdom   United States

THOMSON
DELMAR LEARNING

Instructor's Guide to Accompany Today's Technician: Manual Transmissions and Transaxles, 4E
Jack Erjavec and Don Knowles

Vice President, Technology and Trades SBU:
Alar Elken

Editorial Director:
Sandy Clark

Senior Acquisitions Editor:
David Boelio

Developmental Editor:
Matthew Thouin

Marketing Director:
David Garza

Channel Manager:
Bill Lawrensen

Marketing Coordinator:
Mark Pierro

Production Director:
Mary Ellen Black

Production Editor:
Toni Hansen

Art/Design Specialist:
Cheri Plasse

Technology Project Manager:
Kevin Smith

Technology Project Specialist:
Linda Verde

Editorial Assistant:
Andrea Domkowski

Printed in the United States of America
1 2 3 4 5 XX 08 07 06 05

For more information, contact Thomson Delmar Learning Executive Woods
5 Maxwell Drive, PO Box 8007,
Clifton Park, NY 12065-8007;
or find us on the World Wide Web at
www.delmarlearning.com

Library of Congress Catalog Card Number:

2005015956

ISBN: 1-4018-7754-0

NOTICE TO THE READER

Publisher does not warrant or guarantee any of the products described herein or perform any independent analysis in connection with any of the product information contained herein. Publisher does not assume, and expressly disclaims, any obligation to obtain and include information other than that provided to it by the manufacturer.

The reader is expressly warned to consider and adopt all safety precautions that might be indicated by the activities herein and to avoid all potential hazards. By following the instructions contained herein, the reader willingly assumes all risks in connection with such instructions.

The publisher makes no representation or warranties of any kind, including but not limited to, the warranties of fitness for particular purpose or merchantability, nor are any such representations implied with respect to the material set forth herein, and the publisher takes no responsibility with respect to such material. The publisher shall not be liable for any special, consequential, or exemplary damages resulting, in whole or part, from the readers' use of, or reliance upon, this material.

CONTENTS

Preface   v

ASE Task Correlation Chart   vii

NATEF Task Correlation Chart   xi

ASE Student Checklist   xiv

CHAPTER 1   **Safety**   **1**

Objectives 1 ● Overview 1 ● Reading Assignments 1
● Terms to Know 2 ● Lecture Outline and Notes 2
● Answers to Review Questions 5

CHAPTER 2   **Drivetrain Theory and Typical Shop Procedures**   **7**

Objectives 7 ● Overview 7 ● Reading Assignments 7
● Terms to Know 8 ● Lecture Outline and Notes 8
● Answers to Review Questions 13

CHAPTER 3   **Clutches**   **15**

Objectives 15 ● Overview 15 ● Reading Assignments 15
● Terms to Know 16 ● Lecture Outline and Notes 16
● Answers to Review Questions 20

CHAPTER 4   **Manual Transmissions/Transaxles**   **23**

Objectives 23 ● Overview 24 ● Reading Assignments 24
● Terms to Know 24 ● Lecture Outline and Notes 25
● Answers to Review Questions 34

CHAPTER 5   **Front Drive Axles**   **37**

Objectives 37 ● Overview 37 ● Reading Assignments 37
● Terms to Know 38 ● Lecture Outline and Notes 38
● Answers to Review Questions 46

CHAPTER 6   **Drive Shafts and Universal Joints**   **48**

Objectives 48 ● Overview 48 ● Reading Assignments 48
● Terms to Know 49 ● Lecture Outline and Notes 49
● Answers to Review Questions 54

CHAPTER 7   **Differentials and Drive Axles**   **56**

Objectives 56 ● Overview 57 ● Reading Assignments 57
● Terms to Know 57 ● Lecture Outline and Notes 58
● Answers to Review Questions 66

CHAPTER 8   **Four-Wheel Drive Systems**   **69**

Objectives 69 ● Overview 69 ● Reading Assignments 69
● Terms to Know 70 ● Lecture Outline and Notes 70
● Answers to Review Questions 75

CHAPTER 9   **Advanced Four-Wheel Drive Systems**   **77**

Objectives 77 ● Overview 77 ● Reading Assignments 77
● Terms to Know 78 ● Lecture Outline and Notes 78
● Answers to Review Questions 82

CHAPTER 10 **Drivetrain Electrical and Electronic Systems**   **84**

Objectives 84 ● Overview 84 ● Reading Assignments 84
● Terms to Know 85 ● Lecture Outline and Notes 85
● Answers to Review Questions 90

**Answers to the ASE Practice Examination
(Shop Manual)**   **92**

PREFACE

This Instructor's Guide is provided free of charge as part of the Today's Technician™ series of automotive technology textbooks. This Instructor's Guide is divided into two major parts:

- ASE and NATEF Task Correlation Charts and ASE Student Checklist
- Lecture Outlines and Notes, including Answers to Review Questions

The Lecture Outline and Notes section for each chapter includes the following helpful components:

- Objective Review
- Chapter Overview
- Reading Assignments
- Terms to Know
- Lecture Outline and Notes
- Answers to Review Questions

The ASE and NATEF Task Correlation charts will help you locate the Classroom and Shop Manual pages that are relevant to teaching the ASE/NATEF tasks listed, while the Student ASE Checklist will allow your students to track their progress toward developing competencies in the ASE subject area.

For those seeking a more comprehensive support package for this text, Thomson Delmar Learning is proud to supply its e.resource™. This CD-ROM provides the following instructor resources all on one, easy-to-use disc:

- **Computerized Test Bank**—This test bank offers hundred of questions that can be used to quickly generate exams. It also allows the modification of existing questions and the addition of new questions, as needed.
- **Image Library**—This searchable database of images from the Classroom or Shop Manual can be used to enhance classroom presentations.
- **PowerPoint™ Presentation**—These PowerPoint™ slides provide a visual outline of key concepts in the Classroom and Shop Manuals. They can be further enhanced by importing your own images or images from the Image Library.
- **Worksheets**—These customizable worksheets can be used to assess and reinforce material found in the Classroom and Shop Manuals.
- **Job Sheets**—All Job Sheets in the Shop Manual are provided electronically on the e.resource.™
- **Lecture Outlines and Notes and Answers to Review Questions**—An electronic version of these Instructor's Guide components gives you the flexibility to modify the content to meet your instructional needs.
- **ASE/NATEF Correlation Charts**—These tools provides a quick and easy way to find coverage of the ASE/NATEF tasks in the Classroom and Shop Manuals.
- **Student ASE Correlation Checklist**—This form allows students to track their progress toward developing competencies in the ASE subject area.

If you would like to order the e.resource™, please call Thomson Delmar Learning at 1-800-347-7707 to place an order or for further information.

We hope you find Today's Technician™ to be a useful addition to your automotive classroom!

ASE Task Correlation with *Today's Technician Manual Transmissions and Transaxles, 4E**

*Task list provided by ASE.

	Classroom Manual	Shop Manual
Manual Drivetrain and Axles		
A. Clutch Diagnosis and Repair		
1. Diagnose clutch noise, binding, slippage, pulsation, chatter, pedal feel/effort, and release problems; determine needed repairs.	57	75
2. Inspect, adjust, and replace clutch pedal linkage, cables and automatic adjuster mechanisms, brackets, bushings, pivots, springs, and electrical switches.	68	78
3. Inspect, adjust, replace, and bleed hydraulic clutch slave cylinder/actuator, master cylinder, lines, and hoses; clean and flush hydraulic system; refill with proper fluid.	70	84
4. Inspect, adjust, and replace release (throw-out) bearing, bearing retainer lever, and pivot.	66	105
5. Inspect and replace clutch disc and pressure plate assembly; inspect input shaft splines.	61	95
6. Inspect and replace pilot bearing/bushing; inspect pilot bearing/bushing mating surfaces.	60	104
7. Inspect and measure flywheel and ring gear; inspect dual-mass flywheel damper where required; repair or replace as necessary.	58	98
8. Inspect engine block, clutch (bell) housing, transmission case mating surfaces, and alignment dowels; determine needed repairs.	58	99
9. Measure flywheel surface runout and crankshaft end play; determine needed repairs.	59	98
10. Inspect, replace, and align powertrain mounts.	58	128
B. Transmission Diagnosis and Repair		
1. Diagnose transmission noise, hard shifting, gear clash, jumping out of gear, fluid condition, and type and fluid leakage problems; determine needed repairs.	91	132
2. Inspect, adjust, lubricate and replace transaxle external shifter assemblies, linkages, brackets, bushings/grommets, cables, pivots, and levers.	94	141
3. Inspect and replace transmission gaskets, sealants, seals, and fasteners; inspect sealing surfaces.	92	139
4. Remove and replace transmission; inspect transmission mounts.	92	143
5. Disassemble and clean transmission components; reassemble transmission.	94	145
6. Inspect, repair, and/or replace transmission shift cover and internal shift forks, bushings, bearings, levers, shafts, sleeves, detent mechanisms, interlocks, and springs.	99	161
7. Inspect and replace input (clutch) shaft, bearings, and retainers.	92	155

	Classroom Manual	Shop Manual
8. Inspect and replace main shaft, gears, thrust washers, bearings, and retainers/snap rings; measure gear clearance/end play.	93	157
9. Inspect and replace synchronizer hub, sleeve, keys (inserts), springs, and blocking (synchronizing) rings/mechanisms; measure blocking ring clearance.	84	158
10. Inspect and replace counter shaft, counter (cluster) gear, shaft, bearings, thrust washers, and retainers/snap rings.	93	157
11. Inspect and replace reverse idler gear, shaft, bearings, thrust washers, and retainers/snap rings.	94	156
12. Measure and adjust shaft/gear, and synchronizer end play.	85	159
13. Measure and adjust bearing preload or end play.	82	173
14. Inspect, repair, and replace extension housing and transmission case mating surfaces, bores, bushings, and vents.	92	152
15. Inspect and replace speedometer drive gear, driven gear, and retainers.	90	171
16. Inspect, test, and replace transmission sensors and switches.	265	450
17. Inspect lubrication systems.	92	137
18. Check fluid level, and refill with proper fluid.	82	137

C. Transaxle Diagnosis and Repair

	Classroom Manual	Shop Manual
1. Diagnose transaxle noise, hard shifting, gear clash, jumping out of gear, fluid condition, and type and fluid leakage problems; determine needed repairs.	100	132
2. Inspect, adjust, lubricate and replace transaxle external shift assemblies, linkages, brackets, bushings/grommets, cables, pivots, and levers.	103	141
3. Inspect and replace transaxle gaskets, sealants, seals, and fasteners; inspect sealing surfaces.	92, 100	139
4. Remove and replace transaxle; inspect, replace, and align transaxle mounts and subframe/cradle assembly.	80	143
5. Disassemble and clean transaxle components; reassemble transaxle.	94	162
6. Inspect, repair, and/or replace transaxle shift cover and internal shift forks, levers, bushings, shafts, sleeves, detent mechanisms, interlocks, and springs.	104	161
7. Inspect and replace input shaft, gears, bearings, and retainers/snap rings.	102	155
8. Inspect and replace output shaft, gears, thrust washers, bearings, and retainers/snap rings.	102	157
9. Inspect and replace synchronizer hub, sleeve, keys (inserts), springs, and blocking (synchronizing) rings; measure blocking ring clearance.	102	171
10. Inspect and replace reverse idler gear, shaft, bearings, thrust washers, and retainers/snap rings.	102	156
11. Inspect, repair, and replace transaxle case mating surfaces, bores, dowels, bushings, bearings, and vents.	92, 100	152
12. Inspect and replace speedometer drive gear, driven gear, and retainers.	90	171
13. Inspect, test, and replace transaxle sensors and switches.	265	450

	Classroom Manual	Shop Manual
14. Diagnose differential assembly noise and vibration problems; determine needed repairs.	106	132
15. Remove and replace differential final drive assembly.	106	172
16. Inspect, measure, adjust, and replace differential pinion gears (spiders), shaft, side gears, thrust washers, and case.	106	173
17. Inspect and replace differential side bearings; inspect case.	106	173
18. Measure shaft end play/preload (shim/spacer selection procedure).	100	173
19. Inspect lubrication systems.	100	137
20. Check fluid level, and refill with proper fluid.	100	137
21. Measure and adjust differential bearing preload end play.	106	173

D. Drive Shaft/Half-Shaft and Universal Joint/Constant Velocity (CV) Joint Diagnosis and Repair (Front- and Rear-Wheel Drive)

	Classroom Manual	Shop Manual
1. Diagnose shaft and Universal/CV joint noise and vibration problems; determine needed repairs.	115, 137	191, 233
2. Inspect, service, and replace shafts, yokes, boots, and Universal/CV joints; verify proper phasing.	138	192, 236
3. Inspect, service, and replace shaft center support bearings.	149	237
4. Check and correct drive/propeller shaft balance.	138	250
5. Measure drive shaft runout.	138	252
6. Measure and adjust drive shaft working angles.	129	253
7. Inspect, service, and replace front wheel bearings, seals, and hubs.	129	214

E. Rear-Wheel Drive Axle Diagnosis and Repair

1. Ring and Pinion Gears

	Classroom Manual	Shop Manual
1. Diagnose noise, vibration, and fluid leakage problems; determine needed repairs.	157	268
2. Inspect and replace companion flange and pinion seal; measure companion flange runout.	173	274, 282
3. Measure ring gear runout; determine needed repairs.	174	283
4. Inspect and replace ring and pinion gearset, collapsible spacers, sleeves (shims), and bearings.	166	294
5. Measure and adjust drive pinion depth.	173	301
6. Measure and adjust drive pinion bearing preload (collapsible spacer or shim type).	173	304
7. Measure and adjust differential (side) bearing preload, and ring and pinion backlash (threaded adjuster or shim type).	174	307
8. Perform ring and pinion tooth contact pattern checks; determine needed adjustments.	172	311

2. Differential Case Assembly

	Classroom Manual	Shop Manual
1. Diagnose differential assembly noise and vibration problems; determine needed repairs.	157	270
2. Remove and replace differential assembly.	159	285

	Classroom Manual	Shop Manual
3. Inspect, measure, adjust and replace differential pinion gears (spiders), shaft, side gears, thrust washers, and case/carrier.	160	298
4. Inspect and replace differential side bearings; inspect case/carrier.	164	293
5. Measure differential case/carrier runout; determine needed repairs.	165	290
6. Inspect axle housing and vent.	163	276

3. Limited Slip Differential

	Classroom Manual	Shop Manual
1. Diagnose limited slip differential noise, slippage, and chatter problems; determine needed repairs.	177	320
2. Inspect, drain, and refill with correct lubricant.	166	270
3. Inspect, adjust, and replace clutch (cone/plate) pack or locking assembly.	178	321

4. Axle Shafts

	Classroom Manual	Shop Manual
1. Diagnose rear axle shaft noise, vibration, and fluid leakage problems; determine needed repairs.	185	323
2. Inspect and replace rear axle shaft wheel studs.	186	325
3. Remove, inspect, and replace rear axle shafts, splines, seals, bearings, and retainers.	187	324
4. Measure rear axle flange runout and shaft end play; determine needed repairs.	188	323

F. Four-Wheel Drive/All-Wheel Drive Component Diagnosis and Repair

	Classroom Manual	Shop Manual
1. Diagnose four-wheel drive assembly noise, vibration, shifting, leakage and steering problems; determine needed repairs.	202	346
2. Inspect, adjust, and repair transfer case manual shifting mechanisms, bushings, mounts, levers, and brackets.	204	393
3. Remove and replace transfer case.	197	359
4. Disassemble transfer case; clean and inspect internal transfer case components; determine needed repairs.	206	362
5. Reassemble transfer case; refill with proper fluid.	207	365
6. Check transfer case fluid, level, condition and type.	205	378
7. Inspect, service, and replace front drive/propeller shaft and universal/CV joints.	197	349
8. Inspect, service, and replace front drive axle universal/CV joints and drive/half shafts.	197	350
9. Inspect, service, and replace front wheel bearings, seals, and hubs.	214	355
10. Check transfer case and front axle seals and all vents.	205	348
11. Diagnose, test, adjust, and replace electrical, electronic components of four-wheel/all-wheel drive systems.	211	394
12. Test, diagnose, and replace axle actuation and engagement systems (including: viscous, hydraulic, magnetic, and mechanical).	232	396

The ASE Tasks listed in the correlation chart on the preceding pages are used with the permission of the National Institute for Automotive Service Excellence (ASE), and is current as of 2005

NATEF Task Correlation with *Today's Technician: Manual Transmissions and Transaxles, 4E**

*Task list provided by NATEF.

	Classroom Manual	Shop Manual

Manual Drive Train and Axles

A. General Drive Train Diagnosis

	Classroom Manual	Shop Manual
1. Complete work order to include customer information, vehicle identifying information, customer concern, related service history, cause, and correction.	12	52
2. Identify and interpret drive train concern; determine necessary action.	2	60
3. Research applicable vehicle and service information, such as drive train system operation, fluid type, vehicle service history, service precautions, and technical service bulletins.	11	49
4. Locate and interpret vehicle and major component identification numbers (VIN, vehicle certification labels, calibration decals).	13	52
5. Diagnose fluid loss, level, and condition concerns; determine necessary action.	6	58
6. Drain and fill manual transmission/transaxle and final drive unit.	11	59

B. Clutch Diagnosis and Repair

	Classroom Manual	Shop Manual
1. Diagnose clutch noise, binding, slippage, pulsation, and chatter; determine necessary action.	57	75
2. Inspect clutch pedal linkage, cables, automatic adjuster mechanisms, brackets, bushings, pivots, and springs; perform necessary action.	68	78
3. Inspect hydraulic clutch slave and master cylinders, lines, and hoses; determine necessary action.	70	84
4. Inspect release (throw-out) bearing, lever, and pivot; determine necessary action.	66	105
5. Inspect and replace clutch pressure plate assembly and clutch disc.	61	95
6. Bleed clutch hydraulic system.	70	87
7. Inspect, remove or replace pilot bearing or bushing (as applicable).	60	104
8. Inspect flywheel and ring gear for wear and cracks, determine necessary action.	58	98
9. Inspect engine block, clutch (bell) housing, transmission/transaxle case mating surfaces, and alignment dowels; determine necessary action.	58	99
10. Measure flywheel runout and crankshaft endplay; determine necessary action.	59	98

C. Transmission/Transaxle Diagnosis and Repair

	Classroom Manual	Shop Manual
1. Remove and reinstall transmission/transaxle.	80	143
2. Disassemble, clean, and reassemble transmission/transaxle components.	94	145
3. Inspect transmission/transaxle case, extension housing, case mating surfaces, bores, bushings, and events; perform necessary action.	92	152

	Classroom Manual	Shop Manual
4. Diagnose noise, hard shifting, jumping out of gear, and fluid leakage concerns; determine necessary action.	91	132
5. Inspect, adjust, and reinstall shift linkages, brackets, bushings, cables, pivots, and levers.	94	141
6. Inspect and reinstall powertrain mounts.	80	128
7. Inspect and replace gaskets, seals, and sealants; inspect sealing surfaces.	92	139
8. Remove and replace transaxle final drive.	80	143
9. Inspect, adjust, and reinstall shift cover, forks, levers, grommets, shafts, sleeves, detent mechanism, interlocks, and springs.	103	141
10. Measure endplay or preload (shim or spacer selection procedure) on transmission/transaxle shafts; perform necessary action.	82	173
11. Inspect and reinstall synchronizer hub, sleeve, keys (inserts), springs, and blocking rings.	85	159
12. Inspect and reinstall speedometer drive gear, driven gear, vehicle speed sensor (VSS), and retainers.	90	171
13. Diagnose transaxle final drive assembly noise and vibration concerns; determine necessary action.	100	132
14. Remove, inspect, measure, adjust, and reinstall transaxle final drive pinion gears (spiders), shaft, side gears, side bearings, thrust washers, and case assembly.	106	173
15. Inspect lubrication devices (oil pump or slingers); perform necessary action.	100	137
16. Inspect, test, and replace transmission/transaxle sensors and switches.	265	450

D. Drive Shaft and Half Shaft, Universal and Constant-Velocity (CV) Joint Diagnosis and Repair

	Classroom Manual	Shop Manual
1. Diagnose constant-velocity (CV) joint noise and vibration concerns; determine necessary action.	115	191
2. Diagnose universal joint noise and vibration concerns; perform necessary action.	138	233
3. Remove and replace front wheel drive (FWD) front wheel bearing.	129	214
4. Inspect, service, and replace shafts, yokes, boots, and CV joints.	138	236
5. Inspect, service, and replace shaft center support bearings.	149	237
6. Check shaft balance and phasing; measure shaft runout; measure and adjust driveline angles.	138	252

E. Drive Axle Diagnosis and Repair

1. Ring and Pinion Gears and Differential Case Assembly

	Classroom Manual	Shop Manual
1. Diagnose noise and vibration concerns; determine necessary action.	157	268
2. Diagnose fluid leakage concerns; determine necessary action.	158	275
3. Inspect and replace companion flange and pinion seal; measure companion flange runout.	173	274
4. Inspect ring gear and measure runout; determine necessary action.	174	283
5. Remove, inspect, and reinstall drive pinion and ring gear, spacers, sleeves, and bearings.	166	294
6. Measure and adjust drive pinion depth.	173	301

	Classroom Manual	Shop Manual
7. Measure and adjust drive pinion bearing preload.	173	304
8. Measure and adjust side bearing preload and ring and pinion gear total backlash and backlash variation on a differential carrier assembly (threaded cup or shim types).	174	307
9. Check ring and pinion tooth contact patterns; perform necessary action.	172	311
10. Disassemble, inspect, measure, and adjust or replace differential pinion gears (spiders), shaft, side gears, side bearings, thrust washers, and case.	160	298
11. Reassemble and reinstall differential case assembly; measure runout; determine necessary action.	165	294
2. Limited Slip Differential		
1. Diagnose noise, slippage, and chatter concerns; determine necessary action.	177	320
2. Clean and inspect differential housing; refill with correct lubricant.	166	270
3. Inspect and reinstall clutch (cone or plate) components.	178	321
4. Measure rotating torque; determine necessary action.	179	321
3. Drive Axle Shaft		
1. Diagnose drive axle shafts, bearings, and seals for noise, vibration, and fluid leakage concerns; determine necessary action.	185	323
2. Inspect and replace drive axle shaft wheel studs.	186	325
3. Remove and replace drive axle shafts.	187	324
4. Inspect and replace drive axle shaft seals, bearings, and retainers.	188	325
5. Measure drive axle flange runout and shaft endplay; determine necessary action.	188	323

F. Four-wheel Drive/All-wheel Drive Component Diagnosis and Repair

	Classroom Manual	Shop Manual
1. Diagnose noise, vibration, and unusual steering concerns; determine necessary action.	202	346
2. Inspect, adjust, and repair shifting controls (mechanical, electrical, and vacuum), bushings, mounts, levers, and brackets.	204	393
3. Remove and reinstall transfer case.	197	359
4. Disassemble, service, and reassemble transfer case and components.	206	362
5. Inspect front-wheel bearings and locking hubs; perform necessary action.	214	371
6. Check drive assembly seals and vents; check lube level.	205	348
7. Diagnose, test, adjust, and replace electrical/electronic components of four-wheel drive systems.	211	394

ASE STUDENT CHECKLIST

Manual Drive Train and Axles

A. Clutch Diagnosis and Repair

☑ **Instructor Check & Date**

1. Diagnose clutch noise, binding, slippage, pulsation, chatter, pedal feel/effort, and release problems; determine needed repairs.

2. Inspect, adjust, and replace clutch pedal linkage, cables and automatic adjuster mechanisms, brackets, bushings, pivots, springs, and electrical switches.

3. Inspect, adjust, replace, and bleed hydraulic clutch slave cylinder actuator, master cylinder, lines, and hoses; clean and flush hydraulic system; refill with proper fluid.

4. Inspect, adjust, and replace release (throw-out) bearing, bearing retainer, lever, and pivot.

5. Inspect and replace clutch disc and pressure plate assembly; inspect input shaft splines.

6. Inspect and replace pilot bearing/bushing; inspect pilot bearing/bushing mating surfaces.

7. Inspect and measure flywheel and ring gear; inspect dual-mass flywheel damper where required; repair or replace as necessary.

8. Inspect engine block, clutch (bell) housing, transmission case mating surfaces, and alignment dowels; determine needed repairs.

9. Measure flywheel surface runout and crankshaft end play; determine needed repairs.

10. Inspect, replace, and align powertrain mounts.

B. Transmission Diagnosis and Repair

☑ **Instructor Check & Date**

1. Diagnose transmission noise, hard shifting, gear clash, jumping out of gear, fluid condition, and type and fluid leakage problems; determine needed repairs.

2. Inspect, adjust, lubricate and replace transaxle external shifter assemblies, linkages, brackets, bushings/grommets, cables, pivots, and levers.

3. Inspect and replace transmission gaskets, sealants, seals, and fasteners; inspect sealing surfaces.

4. Remove and replace transmission; inspect transmission mounts.

5. Disassemble and clean transmission components; reassemble transmission.

6. Inspect, repair, and/or replace transmission shift cover and internal shift forks, bushings, bearings, levers, shafts, sleeves, detent mechanisms, interlocks, and springs.

7. Inspect and replace input (clutch) shaft, bearings, and retainers.

8. Inspect and replace main shaft, gears, thrust washers, bearings, and retainers/snap rings; measure gear clearance/end play.

9. Inspect and replace synchronizer hub, sleeve, keys (inserts), springs, and blocking (synchronizing) rings/mechanisms; measure blocking ring clearance.

10. Inspect and replace counter shaft, counter (cluster) gear, shaft, bearings, thrust washers, and retainers/snap rings.

11. Inspect and replace reverse idler gear, shaft, bearings, thrust washers, and retainers/snap rings.

12. Measure and adjust shaft/gear, and synchronizer end play.

13. Measure and adjust bearing preload or end play.

14. Inspect, repair, and replace extension housing and transmission case mating surfaces, bores, bushings, and vents.

15. Inspect and replace speedometer drive gear, driven gear, and retainers.

16. Inspect, test, and replace transmission sensors and switches.

17. Inspect lubrication systems.

18. Check fluid level, and refill with proper fluid.

C. Transaxle Diagnosis and Repair   ☑ Instructor Check & Date

1. Diagnose transaxle noise, hard shifting, gear clash, jumping out of gear, fluid condition, and type, and fluid leakage problems; determine needed repairs.

2. Inspect, adjust, lubricate and replace transaxle external shift assemblies, linkages, brackets, bushings/grommets, cables, pivots, and levers.

3. Inspect and replace transaxle gaskets, sealants, seals, and fasteners; inspect sealing surfaces.

4. Remove and replace transaxle; inspect, replace, and align transaxle mounts and subframe/cradle assembly.

5. Disassemble and clean transaxle components; reassemble transaxle.

6. Inspect, repair, and/or replace transaxle shift cover and internal shift forks, levers, bushings, shafts, sleeves, detent mechanisms, interlocks, and springs.

7. Inspect and replace input shaft, gears, bearings, and retainers/snap rings.

8. Inspect and replace output shaft, gears, thrust washers, bearings, and retainers/snap rings.

9. Inspect and replace synchronizer hub, sleeve, keys (inserts), springs, and blocking (synchronizing) rings; measure blocking ring clearance and slot dimensions.

10. Inspect and replace reverse idler gear, shaft, bearings, thrust washers, and retainers/snap rings.

11. Inspect, repair, and replace transaxle case mating surfaces, bores, dowels, bushings, bearings, and vents.

12. Inspect and replace speedometer drive gear, driven gear, and retainers.

13. Inspect, test, and replace transaxle sensors and switches.

14. Diagnose differential assembly noise and vibration problems; determine needed repairs.

15. Remove and replace differential final drive assembly.

16. Inspect, measure, adjust and replace differential pinion gears (spiders), shaft, side gears, thrust washers, and case.

17. Inspect and replace differential side bearings; inspect case.

18. Measure shaft end play/preload (shim/spacer selection procedure).

19. Inspect lubrication systems.

20. Check fluid level, and refill with proper fluid.

21. Measure and adjust differential bearing preload/end play.

D. Drive Shaft/Half-Shaft and Universal Joint/Constant Velocity (CV) Joint Diagnosis and Repair (Front- and Rear-Wheel Drive)

☑ **Instructor Check & Date**

1. Diagnose shaft and Universal/CV joint noise and vibration problems; determine needed repairs.

2. Inspect, service, and replace shafts, yokes, boots, and Universal/CV joints; verify proper phasing.

3. Inspect, service, and replace shaft center support bearings.

4. Check and correct drive/propeller shaft balance.

5. Measure drive shaft runout.

6. Measure and adjust drive shaft working angles.

7. Inspect, service, and replace front wheel bearings, seals, and hubs.

E. Rear-Wheel Drive Axle Diagnosis and Repair

☑ **Instructor Check & Date**

1. Ring and Pinion Gears

1. Diagnose noise, vibration, and fluid leakage problems; determine needed repairs.

2. Inspect and replace companion flange and pinion seal; measure companion flange runout.

3. Measure ring gear runout; determine needed repairs.

4. Inspect and replace ring and pinion gearset, collapsible spacers, sleeves (shims), and bearings.

5. Measure and adjust drive pinion depth.

6. Measure and adjust drive pinion bearing preload (collapsible spacer or shim type).

7. Measure and adjust differential (side) bearing preload, and ring and pinion backlash (threaded adjuster or shim type).

8. Perform ring and pinion tooth contact pattern checks; determine needed adjustments.

2. Differential Case Assembly

1. Diagnose differential assembly noise and vibration problems; determine needed repairs.

2. Remove and replace differential assembly.

3. Inspect, measure, adjust and replace differential pinion gears (spiders), shaft, side gears, thrust washers, and case/carrier.

4. Inspect and replace differential side bearings; inspect case/carrier.

5. Measure differential case/carrier runout; determine needed repairs.

6. Inspect axle housing and vent.

3. Limited-Slip Differential

    1. Diagnose limited-slip differential noise, slippage, and chatter problems; determine needed repairs.

    2. Inspect, drain, and refill with correct lubricant.

    3. Inspect, adjust, and replace clutch (cone/plate) pack or locking assembly.

4. Axle Shafts

    1. Diagnose rear axle shaft noise, vibration, and fluid leakage problems; determine needed repairs.

    2. Inspect and replace rear axle shaft wheel studs.

    3. Remove, inspect, and replace rear axle shafts, splines, seals, bearings, and retainers.

    4. Measure rear axle flange runout and shaft end play; determine needed repairs.

F. Four-Wheel Drive/All-Wheel Drive Component Diagnosis and Repair

☑ **Instructor Check & Date**

    1. Diagnose drive assembly noise, vibration, shifting, leakage, and steering problems; determine needed repairs.

    2. Inspect, adjust, and repair transfer case manual shifting mechanisms, bushings, mounts, levers, and brackets.

    3. Remove and replace transfer case.

    4. Disassemble transfer case; clean and inspect internal transfer case components; determine needed repairs.

    5. Reassemble transfer case; refill with proper fluid.

    6. Check transfer case fluid, level, condition and type.

    7. Inspect, service, and replace front drive/propeller shaft and universal/CV joints.

    8. Inspect, service, and replace front drive axle universal/CVjoints and drive/half shafts.

    9. Inspect, service, and replace front wheel bearings, seals, and hubs.

    10. Check transfer case and front axle seals and all vents.

    11. Diagnose, test, adjust, and replace electrical, electronic components of four-wheel/all-wheel drive systems.

    12. Test, diagnose, and replace axle actuation and engagement systems (including: viscous, hydraulic, magnetic, and mechanical).

Manual Drive Trains and Axles

Upon completion and review of this chapter, the student should be able to:

1. Identify the major components of a vehicle's drive train.

2. State and understand the purpose of a transmission.

3. Describe the difference between a transmission and a transaxle.

4. Describe the construction and operation of CVTs.

5. State and understand the purpose of a clutch assembly.

6. Describe the difference between a typical FWD and RWD car.

7. Describe the construction of a drive shaft.

8. State and understand the purpose of U- and CV-joints.

9. State and understand the purpose of a differential.

10. Identify and describe the various gears used in modern drive trains.

11. Identify and describe the various bearings used in modern drive trains.

Overview

This chapter describes the basic major components in manual drive trains and explains the basic purpose of each component. The basic design and purpose of minor drive train components such as gears and bearings are explained. Various drive train configurations are explained.

Reading Assignments

Classroom Manual, pages 1–23

Terms to Know

All-wheel drive (AWD)
Ball bearing
Bevel gear
Bushing
Clutch
Constant velocity (CV) joints
Continuously variable transmission (CVT)
Differential
Drive line

Drive shaft
Drive train
End play
Engine torque
Flywheel
Four-wheel drive (4WD)
Front-wheel drive (FWD)
Helical gear
Horsepower
Hypoid gear
Idler gears
Journal

Radial loads
Rear-wheel drive (RWD)
Roller bearing
Spur gear
Thrust bearings
Torque
Transaxle
Transfer case
Universal joints
Worm gear

Lecture Outline and Notes

I. Objectives

Review the chapter's objectives.

II. Introduction

The purpose of the drive train is explained and various components in the drive train are discussed. Types of drive trains are described. The general purpose of the engine is explained, and a discussion of engine torque is included. Basic transmission purpose and types of transmissions are described. The chapter includes a description of clutch purpose and design. Information is provided on drive lines for various types of vehicles. Differentials and axles are explained, and a basic explanation of four-wheel drive systems is provided. Various types of bearings and gears are described.

III. Engine

A. Explain the basic engine purpose, and define engine torque.

1. The engine develops rotary motion, or torque, that is multiplied through the drive train to move the vehicle under a variety of conditions.

2. Engine torque is the turning action of the engine crankshaft.

IV. Transmissions

A. Describe the basic purpose of a transmission.

1. The transmission transmits engine torque through various gear ratios to the drive wheels.

B. Explain basic transmission classifications and designs.

1. Transmissions are classified as transmissions or transaxles, manual or automatic.

2. Automatic transmissions use a torque converter and planetary gears to change gear ratios automatically. Manual transmissions are an assembly of gears and shafts that provide driver-controlled gear ratio changing or shifting.

C. Explain the difference between the design of a transaxle and transmission.

1. A transmission is connected to a separate differential, whereas, in a transaxle, the transmission and differential are combined.

D. Describe the basic design of a continuously variable transmission.

1. Continuously variable transmissions use an expansion pulley and a conventional pulley, coupled by a drive belt to provide gear ratio changes.

V. Clutch

A. Explain the basic purpose of the clutch and its components.

1. The clutch connects and disconnects the engine and the manual transmission or transaxle.

2. The clutch assembly contains a flywheel, clutch disc, pressure plate, clutch release bearing, and clutch linkage.

VI. Drive line

A. Describe the drive line configurations for RWD, FWD, 4WD, and AWD.

1. On RWD vehicles, the drive line contains a drive shaft connected between the transmission and the differential. Universal joints are positioned at each end of the drive shaft to allow smooth drive shaft rotation and changes in drive shaft angles.

2. In a typical 4WD vehicle based on a RWD configuration, a transfer case is mounted on the rear of the transmission, and a second drive shaft is connected to the front differential.

3. If the 4WD vehicle is based on a FWD configuration, a drive shaft is connected from the transaxle output to the rear differential.

4. An AWD vehicle is similar to a 4WD except, in the AWD system, the vehicle is continually in AWD and the driver has no control over the system operation.

VII. Differentials

A. Explain the basic purpose of a differential.

1. The differential acts as a final gear reduction and allows variations in drive wheel speeds when the vehicle is turning a corner.

VIII. Driving Axles

A. Describe the basic drive axle configurations in RWD and FWD vehicles.

1. Driving axles connect the differential side gears to the drive wheels in RWD vehicles. In FWD vehicles, the driving axles connect the differential side gears to the front wheel hubs.

2. In FWD vehicles, a CV joint is mounted near each end of the driving axle. This allows the angles in the drive axle to change as the front wheels move up and down, and turn to the right or left.

IX. Four-Wheel Drive Systems (4WD)

A. Explain the basic power flow and shifting in a 4WD system.

1. In a 4WD system based on a RWD configuration, engine torque is transferred through the transmission and transfer case to the front and rear drive shafts. Engine torque is then supplied to the front and rear differentials and the front and rear wheels.

2. Electric or manual shift controls in the passenger compartment allow the driver to shift from 2WD to 4WD, and from 4WD-High to 4WD-Low.

X. Types of Gears

A. Describe various gear types and classifications.

1. Gears may be classified as spur, helical, or bevel gears.

2. Spur gears have teeth in parallel with the center of the gear. Helical gears have teeth that are twisted at an angle in relation to the gear center.

3. Bevel gears are cone-shaped with the top cut off.

4. Gears may also be classified as hypoid or worm gears. In a hypoid gear, the pinion drive gear is mounted below the center of the ring gear. A worm gear is shaped like a screw.

XI. Types of Bearings

A. Describe the various types of bearings used in automotive drive trains.

1. Bearing types include bushings, thrust bearings, ball bearings, roller bearings, and tapered roller bearings.

XII. Summary

Review the material covered, emphasizing the main points and key words.

Chapter 1 Classroom Manual Answers to Review Questions

● CLASSROOM MANUAL, PAGES 23–25

Short Answer Essays

1. The primary purpose of the drive train is to connect and disconnect the engine's power, to select different gear ratios, to provide a means of reversing the movement of the vehicle, and to supply power evenly to the wheels while the vehicle is making a turn.
2. A limited-slip differential sends torque to the wheel with traction. Normal differentials send most of the torque to the wheel that has the least resistance or traction.
3. An idler gear is used to reduce or increase rotational speeds, and to reverse the direction of rotation. If three gears were connected, the center gear would be considered an idler gear.
4. Transmissions are equipped with different forward gear ratios to allow for a changing amount of torque being delivered to the drive wheels. The gear ratios also allow the engine to operate in its maximum torque curve, increasing the overall efficiency of the drive train.
5. The primary differences between a transaxle and a transmission are that a transaxle has all of the drive train parts housed in a single unit. A transmission is located on the rear of an engine and all other drive train components extend to the rear of the vehicle. Power is supplied to the rear wheels.
6. A U-joint and CV joint allow the drive line to transmit power through the drive line in spite of the fact that the drive line angles are properly aligned and are constantly changing.
7. The differential receives torque from the transmission, where it multiplies the torque in proportion to the gear ratio of the ring gear and pinion. It also transmits power around a corner to the rear wheels.
8. The purpose of a clutch is to provide a smooth engagement and disengagement of the engine's power to the drive train. The clutch consists of a flywheel, pressure plate, and clutch disc. The clutch disc is connected to the transmission's input shaft. The pressure plate applies pressure on the clutch disc that is sandwiched between the pressure plate and the flywheel, causing it to rotate with the flywheel.
9. The kinds of gears that are commonly found in automobiles are straight spur gears, helical gears, bevel gears, spiral bevel gears, and hypoid gears.
10. Ball- and roller-type bearings are used wherever friction must be minimized.

Fill-in-the-Blanks

1. Clutch, transmission, drive axles
2. Engine torque
3. Multiply
4. 4WD vehicles, full-time, all-wheel drive
5. Drive line
6. Bushing
7. Third gear
8. Pressure plate, clutch disc
9. Transaxle
10. Drive shaft

Multiple Choice

1. C
2. C
3. C
4. C
5. B
6. C
7. B
8. B
9. C
10. A

Safety

Upon completion and review of this chapter, the student should be able to:

1. Explain how safety procedures are part of professional behavior.

2. Explain basic principles of personal safety, including protective eye wear, clothing, gloves, shoes, and hearing protection.

3. Inspect equipment and tools for unsafe conditions.

4. Properly work around batteries.

5. Understand the importance of safety and accident prevention in an automotive shop.

6. Explain the procedures and precautions for safely using tools and equipment.

7. Explain the precautions that need to be followed to safely raise a vehicle on a lift.

8. Properly lift heavy objects.

9. Explain the procedures for responding to an accident.

10. Recognize fire hazards.

11. Extinguish the common variety of fires.

12. Identify substances that could be regarded as hazardous materials.

13. Describe the purpose of the laws concerning hazardous wastes and materials, including the Right-To-Know Laws.

Overview

This chapter discusses automotive shop safety. Practicing safety is a mark of professionalism. Safety aspects discussed here include dress, tool, equipment maintenance, fire safety, safe handling of batteries and hazardous materials, and accident response.

Reading Assignments

Shop Manual, pages 1–23

Terms to Know

Blood-borne pathogens
Carbon monoxide (CO)
Caustic
Class A fire
Class B fire
Class C fire
Class D fire
Corrosivity

EP Toxicity
Flammability
Hazardous waste
Hydrocarbon
Ignitability
Material Safety Data Sheet (MSDS)

Occupational Safety and Health Administration (OSHA)
Reactivity
Shank
Volatility

Lecture Outline and Notes

I. Objectives

Review the chapter's objectives.

II. Introduction

The chapter discusses personal safety, including proper work habits and attitude. Fire hazards such as gasoline, diesel fuel, solvents, and oily rags are described, and the proper fire extinguisher for various types of fires is explained. The proper use of a fire extinguisher is detailed. Precautions related to rotating pulleys and belts are described. Tool and equipment safety is explained as it relates to hand tools, power tools, compressed air equipment, vehicle lifts, jacks and jack stands, chain hoists and cranes, and cleaning equipment. This chapter includes a discussion of battery safety, vehicle operation, proper lifting and carrying procedures, and shop accident prevention. Hazardous materials are explained including the Right-To-Know Laws and hazardous waste disposal procedures.

III. Personal Safety

A. Explain the precautions you must take to protect yourself when working in the automotive shop.

B. Identify proper eye protection.

C. Describe the proper clothing to be worn in an automotive shop.

D. Explain proper foot, hand, ear, and respiratory protection.

IV. Fire Hazards and Prevention

A. Explain the fire hazards created by gasoline, diesel fuel, solvents, and oily rags in the shop.

B. Describe the various types of fires and the proper type of fire extinguisher required to extinguish each type of fire.

C. Explain the proper use of a fire extinguisher.

V. Rotating Pulleys and Belts

A. Describe the precautions to be observed when working near rotating pulleys and belts.

VI. Tool and Equipment Safety

A. Explain the hand tool safety precautions that must be observed.

B. Describe the safety precautions that should be adhered to when operating power tools.

C. Explain compressed air equipment safety precautions.

D. Describe the safety precautions that should be adhered to when operating vehicle lifts.

E. Explain the safety precautions that should be adhered to when using jacks, jack stands, chain hoists, and cranes.

F. Describe cleaning equipment safety precautions.

VII. Batteries

A. Explain the hazards created by batteries, and describe the required battery safety precautions.

VIII. Vehicle Operation

A. Describe the necessary driving rules and safety precautions when driving vehicles in the shop and on the street.

IX. Lifting and Carrying

A. Discuss the proper lifting and carrying procedures that must be observed to reduce the possibility of back and other personal injuries.

X. Accidents

A. Describe the necessary shop housekeeping rules that are required to avoid accidents in the shop, and discuss the procedure to be followed if an accident occurs.

XI. Hazardous Materials

A. Explain the typical personal health hazards present in an automotive shop.

B. Describe the role of OSHA in the health hazard field.

C. Explain the Right-To-Know Laws.

D. Discuss qualities of hazardous waste materials and explain MSDS sheets.

E. Describe typical shop waste materials and discuss the proper disposal procedure for each material.

XII. Summary

Review the material covered, emphasizing the main points and key words.

Chapter 1 Shop Manual
Answers to Review Questions

● SHOP MANUAL, PAGES 23-24

ASE-Style Review Questions

1. A
2. C
3. B
4. C
5. C
6. C
7. C
8. A
9. C
10. C

Drivetrain Theory

Upon completion and review of this chapter, the student should be able to:

1. Describe how all matter exists.

2. Explain what energy is and how energy is converted.

3. Explain the forces that influence the design and operation of an automobile.

4. Describe and apply Newton's laws of motion to an automobile.

5. Define friction and describe how it can be minimized.

6. Describe various types of simple machines.

7. Explain how a set of gears can increase torque.

8. Define and determine the ratio between two meshed gears.

9. Explain the difference between torque and horsepower.

10. Explain Pascal's Law and give examples of where it is applied to an automobile.

11. Explain how heat affects matter.

12. Describe the origin and practical application of electromagnetism.

Overview

This chapter provides the basic theories that are used in automotive systems. Understanding these theories is the basis for becoming familiar with the operation and diagnosis of automotive systems.

Reading Assignments

Classroom Manual, pages 27–54

Terms to Know

Acceleration	Gear	Overdrive
Atoms	Gear ratios	Permeable
Centrifugal force	Heat	Potential energy
Centripetal force	Horsepower	Power
Contraction	Impermeable	Pressure
Deceleration	Inertia	Pulley
Direct drive	Kinetic energy	Solution
Electromagnet	Latent heat	Speed
Element	Lever	Tension
Equilibrium	Load	Velocity
Evaporate	Mass	Weight
Expansion	Matter	Work
Force	Mesh	
Friction	Momentum	

Lecture Outline and Notes

I. Objectives

Review the chapter's objectives.

II. Introduction

This chapter presents basic principles that are absolutely essential basis for the understanding of the complex mechanical and electronic systems on modern automobiles. These basic principles include a study of matter, energy and energy conversion, force, motion and friction, work and torque, basic gear theory, heat, and electricity and electromagnetism.

III. Matter

A. Explain matter.

1. Matter may be a liquid, solid, or gas.

B. Explain elements, atoms, compounds, and molecules.

1. An element contains only one type of atom.
2. An atom is the smallest particle of an element.
3. A compound contains two or more types of atoms.
4. A molecule is the smallest particle of a compound.

C. Describe protons, electrons, and neutrons.

1. Protons are positively charged particles located in the nucleus of each atom.
2. Electrons are negatively charged particles that move in orbits around the nucleus of an atom.

D. Explain evaporation, absorption, and adsorption.

IV. Energy

A. Define and explain energy.

1. Energy is the ability to do work.
2. Kinetic energy is released to do work.
3. Potential energy is stored energy.

B. Define energy conversion.

1. Energy conversion occurs when one form of energy is changed to another form.

C. Describe examples of the following types of energy conversion.

1. Chemical to thermal energy conversion.
2. Chemical to electrical energy conversion.
3. Electrical to mechanical energy conversion.
4. Thermal to mechanical energy conversion.
5. Mechanical to electrical energy conversion.
6. Electrical to radiant energy conversion.

D. Describe mass, weight, and size.

1. Mass is the amount of matter in an object.
2. Weight is a force, and gravitational force gives mass its weight.
3. The size of an object defines how much space it occupies.

V. Force

A. Explain balanced and unbalanced forces, and define equilibrium.

1. When all forces applied to an object are balanced, the object is in equilibrium.

2. If unbalanced forces are applied to an object, one force is greater than another force applied to the object.

B. Describe centrifugal and centripetal force.

1. When an object moves in a circle, centrifugal force tends to push the object away from the center, and centripetal force tends to move the object toward the center.

C. Define and discuss pressure.

1. Pressure is a force applied against an object.

2. Pressure is equal to the applied force divided by the area over which the force acts.

3. All the principles of force apply to pressure.

VI. Motion

A. Discuss speed, velocity, acceleration, and deceleration as they relate to motion.

1. Speed is the distance an object travels in a specific length of time.

2. Velocity is the speed of an object in a certain direction.

3. Acceleration is the rate of speed increase.

4. Deceleration is the rate of speed decrease.

B. Explain Newton's Laws of Motion and provide examples of how these laws are applied in automotive systems.

C. Discuss friction, lubrication, and rollers.

1. Friction is the force that slows two moving objects or two surfaces that are in contact.

2. Lubrication and rollers are used to reduce friction.

VII. Work

A. Define work and explain simple machines and inclined planes.

1. Work is accomplished when a force moves an object a specific distance.

2. A machine is any device that can be used to transmit a force and, in the process, change the amount of force or the direction of the force.

3. Less energy is required to move a mass up an inclined plane than to lift the mass vertically.

B. Describe how pulleys and levers are used to do work.

1. A single pulley changes the direction of a force, but not its size.

2. A group of pulleys may be used to reduce a force, but the distance increases proportionally.

3. A lever is a device made up of a bar turning about a fixed pivot point.

4. The distance that a lever moves, the effort required to move the lever, and the load depend on the location of the pivot point.

C. **Explain how gear operation relates to work.**

    1. Based on the size of the gears in mesh, the amount of force applied from one gear to the other can be changed.

D. **Describe the relationship between wheels and work.**

    1. Wheels and tires function as rollers to reduce the amount of friction between a vehicle and the road surface.

E. **Define torque and provide examples of how it applies to automotive systems.**

    1. Torque is force that tends to rotate or turn things.

    2. Torque is measured by multiplying the force applied and the distance traveled.

F. **Define and discuss power and horsepower.**

    1. Power is a measurement of the rate at which work is done.

    2. Horsepower is the rate at which torque is produced.

    3. One horsepower is equal to 33,000 foot-pounds of work per minute.

VIII. Basic Gear Theory

A. **Explain basic gear theory.**

    1. Gears apply torque to other rotating parts of the drive train, and gears are used to multiply torque.

    2. As gears with different numbers of teeth mesh, each rotates at a different speed and torque.

    3. Gear ratios express the mathematical relationship of one gear to another when the two gears are meshed.

    4. Gear ratios also express the amount of torque multiplication between two meshed gears.

    5. Gear ratio is calculated by dividing the number of teeth on the driven gear by the number of teeth on the drive gear.

    6. Gear ratio indicates the number of turns the drive gear must complete to obtain one turn of the driven gear.

B. **Describe the basic power flow through each gear in a four-speed manual transmission, and explain how to calculate the gear ratios in each gear and the overall gear ratio.**

IX. Heat

A. **Define and explain expansion, contraction, and latent heat.**

X. Electricity and Electromagnetism

A. **Describe electricity or electron movement, and explain how voltage and resistance control the flow of electrons.**

B. **Describe permanent magnets and electromagnets, and explain how the number of turns and the amount of current flow determine the strength of an electromagnet.**

C. **Explain how electricity is produced by moving a magnetic field across a conductor, or by moving the conductor through a magnetic field.**

XI. Summary

Review the material covered, emphasizing the main points and key words.

Chapter 2 Classroom Manual
Answers to Review Questions

● CLASSROOM MANUAL, PAGES 54–55

Short Answer Essays

1. Newton's first law of motion is called the law of inertia. It states that an object at rest tends to remain at rest and an object in motion tends to remain in motion, unless some force acts on it. When a car is parked on a level street, it remains stationary unless it is driven or pushed. If the gas pedal is depressed with the engine running and the transmission in drive, the engine delivers power to the drive wheels and this force moves the car.

2. Newton's second law states when a force acts on an object, the motion of the object will change. This change in motion is called acceleration and is equal to the size of the force divided by the mass of the object on which it acts. Trucks have a greater mass than cars. Since a large mass requires a larger force to produce a given acceleration, a truck needs a larger engine than a car. An object's acceleration is directly proportional to the force applied to it, and the object moves in a straight line away from the force. For example, if the engine power supplied to the drive wheels increases, the vehicle accelerates faster.

3. Energy is available in one of six forms.
   1. Chemical energy
   2. Electrical energy
   3. Mechanical energy
   4. Thermal energy
   5. Radiant energy
   6. Nuclear energy

4. 1. Chemical to thermal energy—Chemical energy in gasoline or diesel fuel is converted to thermal energy when the fuel burns in the engine cylinders.
   2. Chemical to electrical energy—The chemical energy in a battery is converted to electrical energy to power many of the accessories on an automobile.
   3. Electrical to mechanical energy—In the automobile, the battery supplies electrical energy to the starting motor, and this motor converts the electrical energy to mechanical energy to crank the engine.
   4. Thermal to mechanical energy—The thermal energy that results from the burning of fuel in the engine is converted to mechanical energy, which is used to move the vehicle.
   5. Mechanical to electrical energy—The generator is driven by mechanical energy from the engine. The generator converts this energy to electrical energy, which powers the electrical accessories on the vehicle and recharges the battery.
   6. Electrical to radiant energy—Radiant energy is light energy. In the automobile, electrical energy is converted to thermal energy, which heats up the inside of light bulbs so they illuminate and release radiant energy.

5. Speed is the distance an object travels in a set amount of time. Velocity is the speed of an object traveling in a particular direction.

6. Torque increases when a smaller gear drives a larger gear. This is due to the difference between the distance from the center of the gear to the point where the gear teeth contact the drive gear, and the distance from the center of the driven gear to the point of contact

with the gear teeth. The torque will increase in proportion to the difference in size between the drive gear and the driven gear. It is the basic principle of the lever.

7. Gear ratios are calculated by dividing the number of teeth on the driven gear by the number of teeth on the drive gear, and are expressed as the ratio drive: driven.

8. As heat moves in and out of a mass, the movement of atoms and molecules in that mass increases or slows down. With an increase in motion, the size of the mass tends to get bigger, or expand. This is commonly called thermal expansion. Thermal contraction takes place when a mass loses heat and the atoms and molecules slow down. All gases, and most liquids and solids, expand when heated, with gases expanding the most. Solids expand and contract at a much lower rate.

9. Torque is a force that tends to rotate or turn things, and is measured by the force applied and the distance traveled.

10. When a solid dissolves into a liquid, its particles break away from this structure and mix evenly in the liquid, forming a solution.

Fill-in-the-Blanks

1. Protons, neutrons
2. Force, distance
3. Work
4. Friction
5. Gravitational pull
6. Turning or twisting
7. Distance, shaft
8. Foot-pounds, Newton-meters
9. Driven, drive
10. 33,000, 550

Multiple Choice

1. B
2. D
3. C
4. D
5. D
6. A
7. A
8. A
9. C
10. D

Special Tools and Procedures

Upon completion and review of this chapter, the student should be able to:

1. Describe the use of common pneumatic, electrical, and hydraulic power tools found in an automotive service department.

2. Describe some of the special tools used to service manual transmissions and the driveline.

3. List the basic units of measure for length, volume, and mass in the two measuring systems.

4. Identify the major measuring instruments and devices used by technicians.

5. Explain what the common measuring instruments and devices measure and how to use them.

6. Describe the proper procedure for measuring with a micrometer.

7. Explain the procedure for using and measuring with a micrometer.

8. Describe the measurements normally taken by a technician when working on a vehicle's drivetrain. Describe the different sources for service information that are available to technicians.

9. Describe the different types of fasteners used in the automotive industry.

10. Describe the requirements for ASE certification as an automotive technician and a master auto technician.

Overview

This chapter provides information on power tools, lifting tools, measuring tools, and special tools and equipment used for driveline service.

Reading Assignments

Shop Manual, pages 31–64

Terms to Know

ASE	Feeler gauge	Preload
Backlash	Fillet	Press-fit
Blowgun	Flat rate	Technical service bulletin (TSB)
Bolt head	Grade marks	
Bolt shank	Inclinometer	Thread pitch
Diagnosis	Jack (safety) stands	Torque wrench
Dial indicator	Machinist's rule	Vehicle Identification Number (VIN)
End play	Micrometer	

Lecture Outline and Notes

I. Objectives

Review the chapter's objectives.

II. Introduction

This chapter provides information on various tools such as torque wrenches, power tools, air wrenches, lifting tools, and measuring tools. Tools and equipment that are used for manual transmission and driveline service are also explained. Service manuals and other sources of service information are discussed in this chapter. The chapter includes information regarding various types of automotive fasteners. A basic discussion of gear adjustments, and general vehicle maintenance are included in this chapter. The general diagnostic procedure included in this chapter can be applied to any diagnostic situation. The chapter concludes with a discussion of what to expect when working as an automotive technician, and how to become ASE certified.

III. Torque Wrenches

    A. Explain the importance of fastener torque, and describe four different types of torque wrenches.

IV. Power Tools

    A. Describe the advantage of power tools.

    B. Explain different types of air wrenches.

    C. Describe bench grinder design and explain the safety precautions to be observed when using this piece of equipment.

    D. Explain various types of shop lights, and explain the safety advantage of fluorescent shop lights.

V. Lifting Tools

    A. Describe hydraulic and pneumatic jack design and operation.

    B. Explain safety stand purpose and explain the use of these stands.

    C. Explain hydraulic vehicle lift purpose, design, and safety precautions.

    D. Describe engine hoist design, purpose, and safety precautions.

VI. Measuring Tools

    A. Explain how to use a machinist's rule.

    B. Demonstrate how to read United States Customary System micrometers, both inside and outside types.

    C. Demonstrate how to read metric micrometers, both inside and outside types.

VII. Feeler Gauge

    A. Explain the design and purpose of a feeler gauge.

    B. Describe the design and purpose of a straightedge.

VIII. Dial Indicator

    A. Explain how to read a dial indicator and provide examples of its application.

IX. Manual Transmissions and Driveline Tools and Equipment

    A. Describe the purpose of a portable crane.

    B. Explain proper procedures for attaching the crane to the component being lifted.

    C. Discuss safety precautions related to the use of a portable crane.

    D. Describe the design, purpose, and operation of a transmission jack.

E. Explain the use of typical transaxle removal and installation equipment.

F. Describe the purpose of transmission/transaxle holding fixtures.

G. Describe the design and purpose of hydraulic, electric, air, or hand driven presses.

H. Explain the design and purpose of a blowgun.

I. Describe the design and purpose of gear and bearing pullers, and explain their use.

J. Explain the design and use of bushing and seal pullers and drivers. Describe the design and purpose of axle pullers.

K. Describe the design, purpose, and use of a clutch alignment tool.

L. Explain the design and use of universal joint tools.

M. Describe the design and purpose of an inclinometer.

N. Explain the design and use of retaining ring pliers.

X. Service Manuals

A. Discuss the use of various types of service information, including aftermarket suppliers' guides, general repair specialty repair manuals, flat-rate manuals, computer-based information, and hotline services.

B. Explain how to locate desired information in a service manual.

C. Interpret various VIN numbers.

D. Discuss the various hotline services available and how to use them.

XI. Fasteners

A. Explain USC and metric bolt terminology.

B. Properly identify bolt features, including bolt head, shank, thread pitch, and grade marks.

XII. Basic Gear Adjustments

A. Explain gear backlash by discussing the clearance between two gear teeth.

B. Explain gear end play by discussing the wear on gears or shafts.

C. Describe gear runout and discuss warping or twisting of gears or shafts.

D. Explain the need for properly preloading bearings and gears.

XIII. General Maintenance

A. Discuss the importance of clean lubricant in transmissions and transaxles.

B. Describe various types of transmission/transaxle and differential lubricants, and explain the importance of using the lubricant specified by the vehicle manufacturer.

XIV. Logical Diagnostics

A. Discuss a logical diagnostic procedure and explain the importance of following such a procedure.

XV. Working as an Auto Tech

    A. Discuss compensation, and explain the advantages and disadvantages of the flat-rate system.

    B. Discuss employer-employee relationships, including these topics:

        1. Instruction and supervision

        2. Clean, safe working environment

        3. Wages

        4. Fringe benefits

        5. Opportunity

        6. Fair treatment

    C. Discuss employee responsibilities including these topics:

        1. Regular attendance

        2. Following directions

        3. Responsibility

        4. Productivity

        5. Loyalty

XVI. ASE Certification

    A. Explain the ASE certification process and the importance of this certification to the technician, employer, and the customer.

    B. Discuss how the ASE tests are configured and written.

    C. Explain the various types of ASE questions and the knowledge required to answer the questions correctly.

XVII. Summary

Review the material covered, emphasizing the main points and key words.

Chapter 2 Shop Manual
Answers to Review Questions

● SHOP MANUAL, PAGES 64–65

ASE-Style Review Questions

    1. A
    2. B
    3. B
    4. C
    5. C
    6. B
    7. C
    8. B
    9. C
    10. D

Clutches

Upon completion and review of this chapter, the student should be able to:

Classroom Manual Objectives

1. Understand and define the purpose of a clutch assembly.

2. Understand and describe the major components of a clutch assembly.

3. Understand and describe the operation of a clutch.

4. Understand and define the role of each major component in a clutch.

5. Describe the operation of the various mechanical and cable-type clutch linkages.

6. Describe the operation of a hydraulic clutch linkage.

7. Diagnose clutch-related problems by analyzing the symptoms.

Shop Manual Objectives

1. Diagnose clutch-related problems.

2. Inspect, adjust, and replace clutch pedal linkage, cables and automatic adjuster mechanisms, brackets, bushings, pivots, and springs.

3. Inspect, adjust, repair, and replace clutch slave and master cylinders, and lines.

4. Bleed a hydraulic clutch system.

5. Inspect, adjust, and replace release bearing, lever, and pivot.

6. Inspect and replace clutch disc assembly.

7. Inspect and replace pilot bearing.

8. Inspect, repair, service, or replace flywheel and ring gear.

9. Inspect engine block, clutch housing and transmission case mating surfaces; determine needed repairs.

10. Measure flywheel-to-block runout and crankshaft end play; determine needed repairs.

11. Measure clutch housing bore-to-crankshaft runout and face squareness; determine needed repairs.

12. Inspect, replace, and align powertrain mounts.

Overview

The Classroom Manual provides a detailed description of the automotive clutch assembly. Each component in the clutch assembly is described, and its function and how it relates to the other components in the clutch assembly are discussed. Clutch system operation is covered in detail. Hydraulic and mechanical clutch linkage systems are also covered.

In the Shop Manual, clutch diagnosis, service, and repair are discussed. Clutch slippage, chatter, and noises are covered. In addition, clutch controls and their adjustments are shown. Clutch removal, inspection, and replacement procedures are discussed in detail.

Reading Assignments

Classroom Manual, pages 57–76
Shop Manual, pages 73–109

Terms to Know

Asbestos	Dual-mass flywheel	Pulsation
Belleville spring	Flexible clutch disc	Quadrant
Bleeding	Flexplate	Rigid clutch disc
Blueing	Free-play	Rivet
Chatter	Fulcrum	Semicentrifugal pressure plate
Clutch disc	Gear clash	
Clutch housing	High pedal	Slave cylinder
Clutch release bearing	Hot spots	Slippage
Clutch shaft	Hub	Splines
Cone clutches	Hygroscopic	Total pedal travel
Diaphragm-spring	Master cylinder	Vibration
Dragging	Pawl	

Lecture Outline and Notes

I. Objectives

Review the chapter's objectives.

II. Introduction (Clutch Purpose)

A. Connect Engine to Transmission
Explain how the engine is connected and disconnected from the transmission.

B. Disconnect Engine from Transmission
Explain the need to shift gears, start the engine, and start the vehicle moving from a stopped position.

III. Clutch Diagnosis

A. Diagnostic Procedure
Learn to use sequential procedures to insure complete diagnosis.

1. Define the importance of determining the customer's complaint.

2. Isolate the problem and eliminate all other possibilities.

3. Determine the cause of the problem. Disassembly may be required to find out if the problem is lack of service or faulty parts.

4. Replace or repair, depending on where you work.

5. Test the repair; always check to see if the repair works and if it removes the customer's complaint.

B. Clutch Problems
Explain how most customer complaints can be put under one of the following categories:

1. Slippage
Define and describe what slippage means in a clutch, and how the engine can be heard running faster than the vehicle. During a road check, try to accelerate.

2. Chatter
Define this noise to give an idea of what to look for.

3. Clutch noises
Define other noises, such as a rattling sound of the linkage or of a catalytic converter with bad baffles.

4. Vibrations
Investigate buzzes that might give an idea of what is vibrating.

5. Dragging clutch
A clutch that will not release properly might be due to worn linkages, or the disc is not properly sliding on the transmission input shaft.

6. Pulsating clutch
When the clutch pedal is let out and the pedal feels as if it is moving up and down, the customer is experiencing a pulsating clutch.

7. Binding clutch
In the case of a binding clutch, the pedal comes up against a tight spot that seems to require more pressure.

IV. Clutch System

A. Flywheel
Describe how a flywheel fastens to the back of the engine and balances the pulsations of the engine.

1. Construction
Describe why a flywheel is typically made of steel with a polished surface, has a starter ring, and is fastened to the crankshaft.

2. Operation
Discuss the purposes of a flywheel and how it balances the pulsations of the engine. It is also used for starter gear and to harmonically balance the engine.

3. Dual-mass flywheel
Discuss the different types of flywheels used (both their construction and materials used).

B. Pilot Bearing
Generally, a bearing or bushing is mounted in the flywheel or rear of the crankshaft release or throw-out bearing. Discuss the types and operation of pilot bearings and how they release pressure plates. Discuss how they are sealed bearings and cannot be serviced.

C. Clutch Disc
Describe the construction of a clutch disc, including facings, hubs, wave springs, and torsion springs.

1. Clutch facings
Discuss construction of the disc, the flexible and rigid type, and the need for the different types. Tell how the rigid type is too harsh for passenger vehicle operation.

2. Clutch hub
Discuss why a clutch hub is splined, on what it slides, and how the transmission input shaft works.

3. Wave springs
Explain why wave springs provide smooth operation so that the clutch is gradually engaged.

---

4. Torsional springs

Discuss how torsional springs absorb torque as the clutch engages, and how they make the clutch less grabby.

D. Pressure Plate

1. Facing

Inspect face, springs and levers, and other parts.

2. Cover

Explain drive and driven parts of the clutch.

3. Belleville springs

Explain why this type of spring is used. Emphasize that Belleville springs are cheaper to manufacture and have moving parts.

4. Coil springs

Explain the difference between Belleville and coil springs. Discuss semi-centrifugal clutches and what makes them more effective at high speed.

5. Release levers (fingers)

Explain how to inspect the fingers and where to look for wear.

E. Release Bearing

Review the need for a release bearing and discuss sealed bearings.

1. Construction

Discuss bearings pressed onto a hub and those packaged as a unit.

2. Constant run

Describe who uses constant run bearings and self-adjusting or hydraulic clutches.

3. Clearance type

Explain who uses the clearance type bearing and the manual linkage types.

F. Clutch Linkage

Explain why clutch linkages are needed and why drivers must engage the clutch from inside the vehicle.

1. Lever and rod

Discuss the advantages and disadvantages of levers and rods. Explain the positive connection and problems that wear causes and the need to constantly check adjustments.

2. Cable

Discuss the advantages and disadvantages of cable clutch linkages. Explain cable stretching and the cable self-adjustment feature.

3. Hydraulic

Discuss the advantages and disadvantages of hydraulic linkages. The hydraulic clutch linkage is located in a good position, but there is a problem with leaks.

4. Slave cylinders

Discuss the different types and locations of slave cylinders used, including the concentric slave cylinder.

V. Clutch Linkage Service

A. Lever and Rod

Explain the procedure for servicing rod-and-lever type clutch linkage.

1. Inspection

Inspection involves visual checks for wear and broken parts. Explain the need for constant service and inspections.

2. Adjustment procedures

Always use service manuals for the vehicle being serviced; explain a general adjustment procedure.

B. Cable

1. Inspection

Make visual inspections, looking for frays and wear points that might indicate a failure at a later time. Point out wear points.

2. Manual adjustment

Use the service manual for the vehicle being serviced and describe all adjustments.

3. Self adjusters

Describe the operation of self-adjuster mechanisms and the problems associated with them.

C. Hydraulic

1. Inspection

Visually inspect for leaks or worn spots indicating some problem with parts rubbing together.

2. Service

Explain service and check fluid for free play that is not supposed to be there.

3. Clutch slave cylinder

Discuss the clutch slave cylinder.

4. Hydraulic clutch bleeding

Describe the hydraulic clutch bleeding procedure.

VI. Clutch Operation

A. Engagement

Review clutch operation and discuss the engagement of the clutch.

B. Disengagement

Review the need to have a method of releasing the clutch; discuss correct terms for release and engagement.

VII. Clutch Replacement

A. Disassembly

1. Shop manual procedure

Use the appropriate manual for the vehicle being worked on.

2. Inspection

Explain the reasons for each inspection point and what to work for.

3. Service precautions

Explain precautions that need to be observed when looking for worn parts. Be careful not to damage a good part.

B. Inspections

Look for parts that need to be replaced.

1. Flywheel

Burned spots indicate the clutch has been slipping and waves on the face indicate wear.

2. Pressure plate

Explain how to measure finger height and point out that some heavy-duty clutches have adjustable fingers.

3. Bell housing

Check for out-of-alignment that would cause the transmission to jump out of gear.

4. Clutch disc

Visually inspect wear surfaces and moving parts to find out if the part can be reused. Explain that some shop owners require these parts to be replaced as a set.

5. Release bearing

Show a release bearing, explain why you replace it, and learn why some shop owners want it replaced when other clutch parts are replaced.

6. Release linkage

Look for wear in bushings and eyelets.

7. Transmission and motor mounts

Learn what to look for. Explain that oil causes mounts to deteriorate very quickly.

C. Reassembly

Explain that reassembly procedures usually take longer to ensure everything is assembled correctly.

1. Shop manual procedure

Explain that this is a reverse procedure, except for periodic checks to assure correct assembly.

2. Service precautions

Review service precautions discussed previously.

VIII. Input Shaft Pilot Bearing and Bushings

A. Describe typical pilot bearing and bushing removal and replacement procedures.

IX. Clutch Release Bearing

A. Explain clutch release bearing diagnosis and service procedures.

X. Guidelines for Servicing Clutch Systems

A. Describe the main points when diagnosing clutch systems and servicing all clutch system components.

XI. Summary

Review the material covered, emphasizing the main points and key words.

Chapter 3 Answers to Review Questions

● CLASSROOM MANUAL, PAGES 76–78

Short Answer Essays

1. The purpose of the clutch assembly is to connect and disconnect engine power from the transmission.
2. The major components of the clutch assembly are the clutch housing, flywheel, clutch shaft, clutch disc, pressure plate, release bearing, and clutch linkage.

3. When the clutch pedal is released, the throw-out bearing moves away from the release fingers of the pressure plate. The clutch disc is then squeezed between the flywheel and the pressure plate, and the power from the engine is transmitted from the clutch disc hub to the transmission input shaft. When the clutch pedal is depressed, the throw-out bearing presses on the release fingers of the pressure plate, which releases the clutch disc. All power is then disconnected from the transmission.

4. The coil spring pressure plate and the diaphragm pressure plate have the same role: to squeeze the clutch disc between the pressure plate and the flywheel in order to engage the clutch or to release it. This action allows the disc to transmit or not to transmit power to the transmission. The major difference between the two types of pressure plate is based on the spring used—multiple coil springs versus a single large cone-shaped spring.

5. The major components of a clutch assembly are the flywheel, which provides a friction surface for the clutch disc to press against; and the pressure plate, which is bolted to the flywheel and squeezes the clutch disc against the flywheel. The clutch disc is the driven member of the assembly and is splined to the input shaft of the transmission.

6. The lever-type clutch linkage uses many parts to transfer the movement of the clutch pedal to the release bearing. Among these are the lever, a bell-crank or cross shaft, and linkage components. When the clutch pedal is depressed, the linkage moves the release lever, which presses on the release bearing, causing the pressure plate to release the clutch disc.

7. The cable-type clutch linkage consists of a flexible outer housing anchored at the upper and lower ends. Moving back and forth inside the housing is a braided stainless steel wire cable that transfers pedal movement to the release lever.

8. The hydraulic clutch linkage consists of a master cylinder, hydraulic tubing, and a slave cylinder. Depressing the clutch pedal causes hydraulic pressure to be applied from the master cylinder through the hydraulic tubing to the slave cylinder, which in turn causes the slave cylinder pushrod to move against the release fork and the release bearing.

9. The centrifugal force adds to spring pressure to produce greater holding force against the clutch disc. This design allows for the use of low-tension springs in the pressure plate. Therefore, less pedal effort is required to depress the clutch pedal without a loss of pressure plate clamping force.

10. The flexible clutch disc has torsional dampener springs that circle the center hub of the disc. The purpose of these springs is to absorb power impulses from the engine that would otherwise be transmitted to the transmission gears. A rigid clutch is a solid circular disc without dampener springs to absorb power pulses.

Fill-in-the-Blanks

1. Bell housing
2. Starting motor
3. Input (clutch)
4. Rigid, flexible
5. Clutch disc
6. Dampener (or) torsional
7. Depressed (or) disengaged
8. Throw-out (release) bearing
9. Master cylinder, hydraulic tubing, slave cylinder
10. Spring, wheel (quadrant)

Multiple Choice

1. B
2. A
3. C
4. C

5. D
6. A
7. B
8. D
9. D
10. A

● SHOP MANUAL, PAGES 110–111

ASE-Style Review Questions

1. A
2. C
3. D
4. C
5. C
6. B
7. C
8. D
9. B
10. C

ASE Challenge Questions

1. B
2. A
3. B
4. C
5. A

Manual Transmissions/Transaxles

Upon completion and review of this chapter, the student should be able to:

Classroom Manual Objectives

1. Understand and discuss the purpose and operation of typical manual transmissions.

2. Understand and describe the purpose, design, and operation of a synchronizer assembly.

3. Understand and discuss the flow of power through a manual transmission.

4. Compare and contrast the design and operation of a transmission and a transaxle.

5. Understand and discuss the flow of power through a manual transaxle.

6. Understand and describe how gears are shifted in a manual transmission/transaxle.

7. Identify the accessories controlled by a manual transmission/transaxle.

8. Discuss the importance of gear oil in a manual transmission/transaxle.

9. Understand and describe the basic operation of a continuously variable transmission.

Shop Manual Objectives

1. Diagnose transmission/transaxle noise, hard shifting, jumping out of gear, and fluid leakage problems; determine needed repairs.

2. Inspect and replace transmission/transaxle gaskets, seals, and sealants; inspect sealing surfaces.

3. Inspect, adjust, and replace transmission/transaxle shift linkages, brackets, bushings, cables, pivots, and levers.

4. Remove and replace transmission/transaxle.

5. Disassemble and clean transmission/transaxle components.

6. Inspect, adjust, and/or replace transmission/transaxle shift cover, forks, grommets, levers, shafts, sleeves, detent mechanisms, interlocks, and springs.

7. Inspect and replace transmission/transaxle input shaft and bearings.

8. Inspect and replace transmission/transaxle main shaft, gears, thrust washers, bearings, and retainers.

9. Inspect and replace transmission/transaxle synchronizer hub, sleeve, inserts, springs, and blocking rings.

10. Inspect and replace transmission counter gear, shaft, bearings, thrust washers, and retainers.

11. Inspect, repair, and replace transmission extension housing and transmission/transaxle case, including mating surfaces, bores, bushings, and vents.

12. Inspect and replace transmission/transaxle speedometer drive gear, driven gear, and retainers.

13. Inspect transmission/transaxle lubrication devices.

14. Measure transmission/transaxle gear and shaft end play/preload; (shim/spacer selection procedure).

15. Diagnose transaxle differential case assembly noise and vibration problems; determine needed repairs.

16. Remove and replace transaxle differential case assembly.

17. Inspect, measure, adjust, and replace transaxle differential pinion gears, shaft, side gears, thrust washers, and case.

18. Inspect and replace transaxle differential side bearings.

Overview

The Classroom Manual discusses both the automotive transmission and transaxle. The purposes of transmissions and transaxles are given, and the similarities and differences are discussed in detail. The student is instructed on the importance of understanding transmission power flow, and the importance of how to trace power flow in a transmission or transaxle. Synchronizers are discussed, their individual parts are described, and synchronizer operation is covered.

Students are also introduced to the various shift methods used in manual transmission and transaxles. A short discussion of transmission-operated electrical devices and the importance of the correct transmission lubricant is given. Continuously variable transmission operation is explained.

In the Shop Manual, transmission/transaxle service is discussed. Problem diagnosis and troubleshooting are also covered. Typical transmission and transaxle removal, disassembly, inspection, reassembly and installation procedures are covered in detail.

Reading Assignments

Classroom Manual, pages 79–111
Shop Manual, pages 125–175

Terms to Know

Block synchronizers	Dog teeth	Peening, Pitting, Rolling, Scoring
Center support plate	Gear rattle	Reverse idler gear
Cluster gear	High gear	Shift forks
Clutch gear	Input shaft	Shift rails
Clutch hub	Lapping	Sliding gear
Collar shift	Locking	Spalling
Constant mesh	Lugging	Synchromesh
Continuously Variable Transmission (CVT)	Main shaft	Tail shaft
	Neutral rollover rattle	Torque steer
Counter gear assembly	Output shaft	
Detent notches		

Lecture Outline and Notes

I. Objectives

Review the chapter's objectives.

II. Introduction

Describe the need for transmission/transaxle in a vehicle.

A. Provides Engine with Mechanical Advantage

1. Gear ratios

Explain gear ratios and how they affect engine speed and torque.

2. Torque multiplication

Explain the effects of torque multiplication on engine and vehicle performance.

B. Provides Means to Drive in Reverse

1. Gear rotation

Show how a gear turning in one direction will drive another gear in the opposite direction.

2. Idler gears

Explain the purpose of the reverse idler gear.

III. Types of Manual Transmission/Transaxles

A. Explain various basic types of manual transmissions including sliding gear, collar shift, and synchromesh transmissions.

B. Explain the reasons for transmissions to have various numbers of forward speeds depending on the vehicle application.

IV. Synchronizers

A. Describe synchronizer purpose and mounting location.

B. Explain synchronizer component design including hub, sleeve, blocking rings, tabs, and springs.

C. Describe synchronizer operation.

D. Describe advanced synchronizer designs.

V. Transmission Designs

A. Describe various transmission designs including three-speed, four-speed, five-speed, six-speed, and overdrive units.

VI. Basic Operation of Manual Transmissions

A. Explain the basic operation of a manual transmission including the input shaft, counter gear assembly, reverse idler gear and shift forks.

B. Describe the power flow through a five-speed transmission in neutral, first gear, second gear, third gear, fourth gear, fifth gear, and reverse.

VII. Gearshift Linkages

A. Explain the design, purpose, and operation of gearshift linkages.

VIII. Basic Transaxle Operation

A. Explain basic transaxle operation.

B. Describe transaxle operation in neutral.

C. Explain transaxle operation in the forward gears.

D. Discuss transaxle operation in reverse.

E. Explain the differential operation in a transaxle.

IX. Continuously Variable Transmissions (CVTs)

A. Explain the operation of continuously variable transmissions at various vehicle speeds.

B. Describe methods of CVT controls.

C. Explain various CVT designs.

X. Transmission Identification and Maintenance

A. Identify the transmission manufacturer and transmission type.

B. Locate the transmission identification tag and interpret the transmission number.

C. Explain various types of manual transmission lubricants.

XI. Diagnostics

A. Describe a typical external visual transmission/transaxle inspection.

B. Discuss shift linkage problems.

C. Explain transmission/transaxle problems caused by worn engine mounts, and discuss engine mount replacement procedures.

D. Explain transmission/transaxle lubricant leak locations and leak diagnosis.

XII. Troubleshooting Transmission/Transaxle Problems

A. Discuss other defects that may be the cause of transmission complaints.

B. Discuss general transmission diagnosis including gear rattle, vehicle lugging, and neutral rollover rattle.

C. Explain transmission diagnosis including these problems:

1. Hard shifting and gear clash.

2. Unit will not shift into a certain gear.

3. Unit jumps out of gear.

4. Unit is locked in one gear.

5. Unit exhibits excessive vibration.

6. Transmission noise, knock at low speeds, noise during a turn, clunk during acceleration and/or deceleration.

XIII. In-Car Service

    A. Discuss transmission/transaxle fluid changes.

    B. Discuss transmission rear oil seal and bushing replacement.

    C. Explain linkage adjustments.

    D. Describe speedometer drive gear service.

XIV. Removing the Transmission/Transaxle

    A. Discuss transmission/transaxle removal procedures.

XV. Disassembling the Transmission

    A. Explain transmission disassembly procedures.

XVI. Inspection of Transmission/Transaxle Parts

    A. Explain transmission inspection procedures on these components.

       1. Case.

       2. Extension housing.

       3. Center support plate.

       4. Front bearing retainer.

       5. Bearings.

       6. Gears.

       7. Input shaft.

       8. Reverse gear.

       9. Reverse idler gear.

       10. Counter gear.

       11. Main shaft.

       12. Synchronizer assembly.

       13. Shift forks.

       14. Shift rails.

       15. Interlock plates.

       16. Miscellaneous small parts.

XVII. Cleaning Transmission/Transaxle Components

    A. Discuss transmission cleaning procedures including aluminum case repair and thread repair.

XVIII. Reassembly of the Transmission/Transaxle

    A. Explain transmission reassembly procedures.

XIX. Disassembly of the Differential Case

    A. Describe the proper disassembly and reassembly procedure for the differential case.

    B. Explain the shim selection procedure for differential shims.

XX. Installing the Transmission/Transaxle

    A. Discuss transmission/transaxle installation procedures.

XXI. Summary

Review the material covered, emphasizing the main points and key words.

Chapter 4 Answers to Review Questions

● CLASSROOM MANUAL, PAGES 111–113

Short Answer Essays

1. The purpose of a transmission is to use different gear ratios to provide the engine with a mechanical advantage over the vehicle's drive wheels.

2. The primary purpose of a synchronizer is to equalize the speed of a shaft and gears before they are engaged in order to eliminate gear clashing and allow for smooth changing of gears. It also serves to lock these parts together.

3. The three stages of synchronization are: (1) The sleeve is moved toward the gear by the shifter lever. The movement of the sleeve causes the inserts to press the blocking ring into the cone of the gear. (2) The synchronizer sleeve slips over the teeth of the gear cone. This brings the gear to the same speed as the synchronizer assembly. (3) The sleeve slides over the gear teeth, locking the gear and its synchronizer assembly to the main shaft.

4. The front bearing retainer serves several functions: it houses an oil seal that prevents oil from leaking out the input shaft; it holds the front bearing rigid in the transmission case; and it serves as the sleeve for the throw-out bearing to ride on.

5. Reverse is obtained by the addition of an extra gear in the geartrain, called the reverse idler gear, which causes the reverse gear to rotate in a direction opposite the direction of the forward gears.

6. The transmission and transaxle are practically identical in operation; both provide torque multiplication and allow for synchronized shifting. Transaxles, however, contain the differential gears and are connected directly to the drive axles.

7. The major difference between the differential of a rear-wheel drive (RWD) vehicle and a front-wheel drive (FWD) vehicle is the way power flows. In RWD, power flow changes direction 90 degrees between the ring gear and the pinion. This change in direction is not needed with FWD because the transverse engine location places the crankshaft so that it is rotating in the correct direction.

8. A CVT uses belts and pulleys, rather than gears. Each pulley consists of a pair of cones that can be moved close together or farther apart to adjust the diameter at which the belt operates. The pulley ratios are electronically controlled to select the best overall drive ratio based on throttle position, vehicle speed, and engine speed. Different speed ratios are available any time the vehicle is moving. Since the size of the drive and driven pulleys can vary greatly, vehicle loads and speeds can be changed without changing the engine's speed. One pulley is the driven member and the other is the drive member. Each pulley has a moveable face and a fixed face. When the moveable face moves, the effective diameter of the pulley changes. The change in effective diameter changes the effective pulley (gear) ratio. A belt links the driven and drive pulleys.

9. When first gear is selected, the first and second gear synchronizer engages with first gear. This connects first gear with the output shaft. Since first gear and the input shaft are in

constant mesh, power flows from the input shaft to the output shaft. This causes the output shaft to drive the differential ring gear.

10. Fifth gear in transmissions and transaxles reduces engine rpm at highway speeds, and therefore decreases fuel consumption and engine noise.

Fill-in-the-Blanks

1. Gears, power, drive wheels
2. Transmission, differential, drive axles
3. Hub, sleeve, blocker ring, inserts
4. Input or speed gear
5. Shift forks
6. Main shaft
7. Sliding gear, collar shift, synchromesh
8. Constant mesh, collar shifted
9. Belts, pulleys
10. Gears, shaft

Multiple Choice

1. C
2. A
3. B
4. C
5. C
6. B
7. C
8. A
9. A
10. C

● SHOP MANUAL, PAGES 175–176

ASE-Style Review Questions

1. C
2. D
3. D
4. C
5. B
6. A
7. A
8. C
9. D
10. A

ASE Challenge Questions

1. A
2. B
3. D
4. D
5. A

Front Drive Axles

Upon completion and review of this chapter, the student should be able to:

Classroom Manual Objectives

1. Explain the purposes of a front-wheel drive (FWD) car's drive axles and joints.

2. Understand and describe the different methods used by manufacturers to offset torque steer.

3. Name and describe the different types of CV joints currently being used.

4. Name and describe the different designs of CV joints currently being used.

5. Explain how a ball-type CV joint functions.

6. Explain how a tripod-type CV joint functions.

Shop Manual Objectives

1. Conduct a safe and effective road test to identify axle and joint problems.

2. Diagnose axle shaft and CV joint noise and vibration problems; determine needed repairs.

3. Inspect, service, and replace shafts, boots and CV joints.

4. Inspect, service, and replace FWD front wheel bearings and their hubs.

Overview

The Classroom Manual deals with front-wheel drive axle designs. Although four-wheel drive and rear-wheel drive axle designs are mentioned, the emphasis is on axles used in front-wheel drive vehicles. The purpose of the axle is given and its ability to flex with steering action and suspension jounce and rebound are discussed. Equal and unequal length axles are described. Torque steer is defined and the various methods used to eliminate torque steer on vehicles using unequal length half-shafts are discussed.

The construction of Rzeppa, fixed tripod, double-offset, cross groove, and plunging tripod joints are discussed in detail. The construction of each joint is given. The various types of boots and boot clamps used on CV joints are described. The differences in the wear rates for inboard and outboard joints are explained.

In the Shop Manual, diagnosis of front-wheel drive axle problems is discussed. Proper visual inspection procedures are explained. Axle assembly, axle bearing and boot removal and installation procedures are also covered. The use of proper procedures and tools is stressed. Axle, axle bearing, CV joint and boot inspection, service and repair are explained in detail.

Reading Assignments

Classroom Manual, pages 115–131
Shop Manual, pages 191–225

Terms to Know

Axle shaft	Half-shaft	Rebound
Bellows-type boots	Inboard joint	Rzeppa joint
Cross groove CV joint	Intermediate shaft	Shudder
CV joint	Jounce	Torque steer
Dimpling	Outboard joint	Tripod CV joint
Double-offset joint	Pinch bolt	Universal joint
Eccentric washer	Pinch clamp	Wheel shimmy
Fixed joint	Plunging joint	

Lecture Outline and Notes

I. Objectives

Review the chapter's objectives.

II. Introduction

A. Explain the purpose of the front drive axles.

B. Describe front axle configurations with transversely-mounted and longitudinally-mounted engines.

III. Drive Axle Construction

A. Describe basic drive axle construction.

B. Describe drive axle location on FWD and 4WD vehicles.

C. Discuss basic CV joint location in the FWD system.

D. Explain and illustrate CV joint action as the suspension moves upward and downward.

E. Describe CV joint action when the front wheels are steered to the right or left.

IV. Drive Axles

A. Explain the reason for unequal-length drive axle.

B. Explain the why unequal length drive axles cause torque steer.

C. Discuss the design and advantage of equal-length drive axles.

D. Describe the location and purpose of drive axle damper weights.

E. Discuss drive axle supports.

V. CV Joints

A. Compare CV joints and universal joints, and explain the advantage of CV joints.

VI. CV Joint Boots

A. Explain the result of dirt and moisture entering a CV joint.

B. Describe the purposes of CV joint boots to seal dirt and moisture out and keep the lubricant in the joints.

C. Discuss types of CV joints including OEM style and split boot.

D. Discuss types of boot clamps and high-temperature boots.

VII. Types of CV Joints

A. Explain the location of inboard and outboard CV joints.

B. Describe two types of outboard joints, Rzeppa and fixed CV joint.

C. Explain three types of inboard joints, double offset joint (DOJ), plunging tripod, cross groove plunge joint.

D. Describe the differences between fixed and plunging CV joints, and explain why inboard plunging joints are necessary.

VIII. CV Joint Designs

A. Explain ball-type and tripod-type CV joints.

IX. Outboard CV Joint Designs.

A. Discuss Rzeppa or ball-type CV joints.

B. Explain the inner race mounted on the axle shaft.

C. Describe how the ball bearings work back and forth in the race grooves.

D. Explain the purpose of the cage to hold the balls in proper position.

E. Describe the outer race and explain how it works with the other joint components.

F. Describe a fixed CV joint and where it is located.

G. Explain the hub, trunnion, and outer housing.

H. Explain the operation of the trunnion joint.

X. Inboard CV Joint Designs

A. Define double-offset CV joints and explain how they operate.

   1. Review plunging joint operation.

   2. Describe how the grooves are made longer so the modified Rzeppa joint will work as a plunging joint.

   3. Explain how the 25-degree operating angle allows the joint to operate at a wider angle.

B. Describe the cross groove CV joint and explain how the grooves cross each other in the outer race.

   1. Explain the need for the 22-degree operating angle in the inboard position.

C. Describe the tripod joint, and explain the need for the longer grooves.

D. Review wheel and suspension jounce and rebound.

E. Discuss CV joint wear and explain why the inner joint experiences a slower wear rate compared to the outer joint.

F. Explain why the outer joint is subjected to higher operating angles and increase wear rate.

XI. FWD Wheel Bearings

A. Explain FWD wheel bearing mounting, design, and purpose.

XII. Front Drive Axle Service

A. Describe basic front drive axle service.

XIII. Maintenance

A. Explain basic front drive axle and wheel bearing maintenance.

XIV. Diagnosing FWD Axle Problems

A. Discuss the importance of obtaining information from the customer regarding the vehicle symptoms.

B. Explain driving procedures during front axle diagnosis such as driving in all gears including reverse.

C. Discuss the cause of the following problems:

1. Clicking while turning a corner.
2. Clunking during torque changes.
3. Shimmy or shudder during acceleration.
4. Shudder while coasting.
5. High speed vibration.
6. Growling or humming noise.
7. Bearing noise.

XV. Visual Inspection

A. Explain inspection procedures for wheels, tires, suspension, and brake components.

B. Explain the defects to look for when inspecting front drive axle boots and clamps.

C. Describe the inspection procedures for transaxle seal leaks.

D. Explain the procedure for inspecting transaxle output shaft bushings.

E. Discuss front drive axle inspection procedures.

XVI. Drive Axle Removal

A. Explain the importance of following service manual removal procedures.

B. Describe axle hub nut removal procedure with the vehicle on the shop floor. Do not use an impact wrench for this procedure.

C. Discuss lower ball joint removal procedures.

D. Explain the reason for installing boot protectors, and discuss wheel hub removal procedures including the use of the proper puller on some applications.

E. Describe removal of the inner drive axle joint from the transaxle.

F. Explain the reason for spacer installation in the differential on some applications.

G. Discuss drive axle installation procedures including cleanliness, new axle nut, no impact wrenches, and the use of special tools to pull the drive axle into the hub on some applications.

H. Explain the final torquing and staking of the drive axle nut.

XVII. Bench Inspection

A. Discuss the reason for boot marking in relation to the drive axle shaft.

B. Explain the satisfactory and unsatisfactory joint grease conditions.

C. Describe joint cleaning procedures, and explain joint component inspection for cracks, chips, pits, rust, and wear or dimpling.

XVIII. Service Kits

A. Discuss the contents and installation of drive axle joint service kits.

XIX. General Service Procedures

A. Explain the proper procedure for replacing drive axle boots and clamps.

B. Describe the proper procedure for replacing inboard and outboard CV joints.

XX. FWD Front Wheel Bearings

A. Explain FWD wheel bearing inspection including end play measurement.

B. Describe FWD wheel bearing replacement procedures.

XXI. Summary

Review the material covered, emphasizing the main points and key words.

Chapter 5 Answers to Review Questions

● CLASSROOM MANUAL, PAGES 131–133

Short Answer Essays

1. CV joints allow the driving axles to rotate at a constant speed while transmitting torque regardless of the operating angle of the joint.
2. The difference between a fixed and a plunging joint includes the capability of the plunging joint to move in-and-out, while the fixed joint does not plunge in or out to compensate for changes in length.
3. When conventional U-joints are operating at an angle, the speed of the shaft changes during each revolution. This change in speed causes a vibration or pulsing as it rotates. CV joints turn at the same speed during all operating angles and therefore deliver smooth power to the wheels.

4. The different methods of offsetting torque are: equal length shafts used to reduce torque steer; or, if the shafts are not equal in length, one is usually made thicker than the other; or one axle may be solid while the other is hollow. Combinations of these features would allow both axles to twist the same amount while transmitting torque.

5. Bellows-type boots are installed over each CV joint to retain lubricant and to keep out moisture and dirt.

6. Front-wheel drive wheel bearings allow the axle to rotate evenly and smoothly and keep the axle in the center of the steering knuckle's hub.

7. The Rzeppa is based on a ball-and-socket principle; it has an inner race attached to the axle. The balls and bearing cage are pressed into the outer housing that serves to keep the ball bearings in place as they ride in the grooves of the inner and outer race. The tripod CV joint uses a central hub that has three trunnions fitted with spherical rollers on needle bearings. These spherical rollers, or balls, ride in the grooves of an outer housing that is attached to the axle. Since the balls are not held in a set position in the hub, they are free to move back and forth within the hub.

8. The outer fixed joints typically wear at a higher rate than the inner plunging joints because of the increased range of operating angles to which they are subjected.

9. A small vibration damper is sometimes attached to one half-shaft to dampen harmonic vibrations in the driveline and to stabilize the shaft as it spins.

10. The most common ball-type joint is the Rzeppa, which is based on the ball-and-socket principle. The inner race has several precisely machined grooves spaced around its outside diameter. The bearing cage is pressed into the outer housing and serves to keep the joint's ball bearings in place as they ride in the grooves of the inner race. When the axle rotates, the inner bearing race and the balls turn with it. The balls, in turn, cause the cage and the outer housing to turn with them. The grooves machined in the inner race and outer housing allow the joint to flex. The balls serve both as bearings between the races and as the means of transferring torque from one to the other.

Fill-in-the-Blanks

1. Inboard, outboard; fixed, plunging; ball-type, tripod
2. Thicker, solid, tubular
3. Balls, race, housing
4. Hub, trunnions, housing
5. Outer, inner, increased, angles
6. Plunging
7. Axle shafts, drive shafts
8. Uniform torque, constant speed
9. Non-positive, positive, single retention
10. Equal length

Multiple Choice

1. A
2. B
3. C
4. D
5. A
6. D
7. A
8. C
9. B
10. B

ASE-Style Review Questions

1. A
2. A
3. C
4. C
5. C
6. B
7. C
8. B
9. B
10. B

ASE Challenge Questions

1. D
2. C
3. B
4. B
5. C

Drive Shafts and Universal Joints

Upon completion and review of this chapter, the student should be able to:

Classroom Manual Objectives

1. Understand and describe the purpose and construction of common RWD drive shaft designs.

2. Understand and describe the purpose and construction of common Universal joint designs.

3. Explain the importance of drive shaft balance.

4. Explain the natural speed variations inherent to a drive shaft.

5. Describe the effects of canceling Universal joint angles.

Shop Manual Objectives

1. Diagnose shaft and Universal joint noise and vibration problems and determine needed repairs.

2. Inspect, service, and replace shaft, yokes, boots, and Universal joints.

3. Inspect, service, and replace shaft center support bearings.

4. Check and correct shaft balance.

5. Measure shaft runout.

6. Measure and adjust shaft angles.

Overview

The Classroom Manual explains the need for the drive shaft to be able to transmit torque through angle and length changes. Students are introduced to the concept of operating angles and learn why a flexibly jointed drive shaft is necessary. The parts of the typical drive shaft are listed and explained. Critical speed is defined and shaft designs for eliminating vibrations are given.

Hotchkiss, torque tube, and steel rope drive shafts are defined. The Hotchkiss-type drive shaft is explained in detail and the individual parts—shaft, Universal joints, and slip joints—are named. Both Cardan and double Cardan U-joints are fully explained.

The chapter also explains Universal joint acceleration and deceleration forces, and the need for canceling angles and drive shaft phasing.

In the Shop Manual, diagnosing drive shaft problems, including road testing, vibrations, noises, and causes of failure, is discussed. Drive shaft service, including inspection, removal, disassembly, and rebuilding joints, is covered in detail. The shop manual also covers drive shaft vibration correction, including balancing. Measuring and adjusting drive shaft angles is also discussed.

Reading Assignments

Classroom Manual, pages 135–151
Shop Manual, pages 233–257

Terms to Know

Amplitude

Canceling angles

Cardan/Spicer
Universal joint

Double Cardan CV joint

Drive shaft

Ellipse

Frequency

Hertz

Hotchkiss drive

Inclinometer

In-phase

Installation angle

Magneto-rheological (MR)
fluid

Operating angle

Propeller shaft

Slip joint

Torque tube

Total runout

Yoke

Zerk fitting

Lecture Outline and Notes

I. Objectives

Review the chapter's objectives.

II. Introduction

A. Discuss the purpose of the drive shaft.

B. Describe drive shaft construction and configuration on two-wheel drive and four-wheel drive vehicles.

III. Drive Shaft Construction

A. Describe the reason for universal joints on each end of the drive shaft.

B. Discuss drive shaft frequency and vibration.

C. Describe the need for drive shaft balance, and explain various methods of balance.

D. Explain different drive shaft materials and the advantage of each.

IV. Types of Drive Shafts

A. Describe various types of drive shaft configuration including, Hotchkiss drive, torque tube, and flexible tube.

V. Universal Joints

A. Describe basic cardan universal joint design including the cross and roller construction and joint retention methods.

B. Explain the basic operation of a cardan universal joint, and describe the reason for a drive shaft yoke.

C. Explain the speed changes in output shaft rotation as a drive shaft rotates.

D. Explain the drive shaft operating angle.

E. Describe drive shaft phasing.

F. Explain drive shaft canceling angles.

VI. Types of Universal Joints

A. Describe different types of single universal joints.

B. Describe double cardan universal joint design and advantages.

C. Explain CV joints.

D. Explain the purpose and design of slip joints.

VII. Center Support Bearings

A. Describe the purpose and design of center support bearings.

B. Explain the purpose of magneto-rheological fluid in the center support bearing housing.

VIII. Diagnosing Drive Shaft Problems

A. Discuss road test purpose and procedure.

C. Explain the cause of unwanted vibrations.

D. Explain frequency, hertz, and amplitude.

E. Discuss the causes of drive shaft vibration at various speeds.

F. Explain the causes of various drive shaft noises squeaking at low speeds, and clunking when the transmission is placed in drive or reverse.

G. Describe the causes of universal joint failure such as system modification, towing, overloading, abrupt gear changes, and off-road operation.

H. Discuss universal joint lubrication.

IX. Drive Shaft Inspection

A. Explain drive shaft inspection procedure including checking for fluid leaks at the transmission output shaft seal, differential pinion seal, and U-joint grease seals.

B. Describe the procedure for checking for U-joint wear.

C. Describe the visual inspection of drive shaft condition including missing weights, dents, dirt accumulation including undercoating, and slip yoke looseness.

X. Removing and Installing a Drive Shaft

A. Explain the drive shaft removal procedure including marking of the drive shaft in relation to the differential yoke prior to removal.

B. Describe the drive shaft installation procedure.

XI. Disassembling and Assembling Universal Joints

A. Describe universal joint disassembly procedures including marking of drive and driven yokes, bearing caps, and trunnions.

B. Discuss universal joint disassembly tools including sockets, a bench vise, C-clamps, and a hydraulic press.

C. Explain universal joint assembly procedures emphasizing the importance of aligning all the index marks.

XII. Double Cardan U-Joints

A. Discuss double cardan U-join disassembly procedures including the importance if index marking all bearing caps in relation to the housing, and removing bearing caps in proper sequence.

B. Discuss centering ball removal procedure.

C. Explain double cardan U-joint assembly procedure.

XIII. Drive Shaft Balance

A. Describe drive shaft balance procedure using hose clamps.

XIV. Drive Shaft Runout

A. Explain drive shaft runout measurement procedure using a dial indicator.

XV. Universal Joint and Shaft Angles

A. Explain the use of an inclinometer to measure drive shaft angle.

B. Describe the adjustment procedure for correcting improper drive shaft angles.

XVI. Summary

Review the material covered, emphasizing the main points and key words.

Chapter 6 Answers to Review Questions

● CLASSROOM MANUAL, PAGES 151–153

Short Answer Essays

1. The purpose of a Universal joint is to permit variations in the driveline angles while transferring torque from the transmission to the drive axles.

2. The methods of reducing drive shaft torsional vibrations are: making the drive shafts as large in diameter as possible, as short as possible, making shafts with cardboard liners, using the tube-in-tube design, and balancing them.

3. U-joint operating angles are determined by the difference between the transmission installation angle and the drive shaft installation angle.

4. When a U-joint is operating at an angle, the driven yoke speeds up and down twice during each drive shaft revolution. This speeding up and down causes a vibration.

5. The speeding up and down of a U-joint is transferred down the drive shaft to the next U-joint. At this U-joint, similar speed changes occur. Since these speed changes take place at times opposite those of the first U-joint, they cancel each other out. Speed fluctuations can only be canceled if the U-joints are on the same plane or are "in phase."

6. The operating angles of the U-joint must be equal to each other and in phase to provide this canceling effect.

7. A single Cardan U-joint uses a spider, four machined trunnions, needle bearings, and bearing caps to allow power flow through slight shaft angles.

8. A double Cardan joint is sometimes called a constant velocity joint because shaft speeds do not fluctuate through various shaft angles. The joint consists of two Cardan joints closely connected by a centering socket yoke. Because of the centering socket yoke, the total

operating angle is divided equally between the two U-joints. Since the U-joints operate at the same angle, speed fluctuations are canceled by the equal and opposite action of the other.

9. A two-piece drive shaft is used on long wheelbase vehicles to reduce torsional vibration.
10. The methods used to retain a U-joint in its yoke are the use of a snap ring, C-clip, bearing plate, thrust plate, wing bearing, bearing cap bolts, U-bolts, and strap.

Fill-in-the-Blanks

1. Seamless steel, Universal joint yokes
2. Output shaft
3. Yokes
4. Balance weights, balance, vibration
5. Front Universal joint
6. Drive shaft, two
7. Torque tube
8. Single, coupled (or double)
9. Spicer, Mechanics, Cleveland
10. Tube-in-tube

Multiple Choice

1. C
2. B
3. A
4. B
5. B
6. D
7. C
8. D
9. B
10. C

● SHOP MANUAL, PAGES 258–259

ASE-Style Review Questions

1. D
2. A
3. C
4. B
5. C
6. C
7. A
8. B
9. C
10. C

ASE Challenge

1. C
2. B
3. D
4. A
5. B

Differentials and Drive Axles

Upon completion and review of this chapter, the student should be able to:

Classroom Manual Objectives

1. Describe the purpose of a differential.

2. Identify the major components of a differential and explain their purpose.

3. Describe the various gears in a differential assembly and state their purpose.

4. Describe the various methods used to mount and support the drive pinion shaft and gear.

5. Explain the need for drive pinion bearing preload.

6. Describe the difference between hunting, nonhunting, and partial nonhunting gear sets.

7. Explain the purpose of the major bearings within a differential assembly.

8. Describe the operation of a limited-slip differential.

9. Describe the construction and operation of a rear axle assembly.

10. Identify and explain the operation of the two major designs of rear axle housings.

11. Explain the operation of a FWD differential and its drive axles.

12. Describe the different types of drive axles and the bearings used to support each of them.

Shop Manual Objectives

1. Diagnose differential and rear axle noise, vibration, and fluid leakage problems; determine needed repairs.

2. Diagnose limited-slip differential noise, slippage, and chatter problems; determine needed repairs.

3. Inspect and replace the companion flange and pinion seal. Measure companion flange runout.

4. Inspect and replace ring gear.

5. Measure ring gear runout; determine needed repairs.

6. Inspect and replace drive pinion gear, collapsible spacers, sleeves, and bearings.

7. Measure and adjust drive pinion depth.

8. Measure and adjust drive pinion bearing preload.

9. Measure and adjust differential (side) bearing preload and ring and pinion backlash (threaded cup or shim type).

10. Measure shaft end play/preload (shim/spacer selection procedure).

11. Perform ring and pinion tooth contact pattern checks; determine needed adjustments.

12. Remove and replace differential assembly and ring gear.

13. Inspect, measure, adjust, and replace differential pinion gears (spiders), shaft, side gears, thrust washers, and case.

14. Inspect and replace differential side bearings.

15. Measure differential case runout; determine needed repairs.

16. Inspect, flush, and refill a limited-slip differential with correct lubricant.

17. Inspect, adjust, and replace limited-slip clutch (cone/plate) pack.

18. Inspect and replace rear axle shaft wheel studs.

19. Remove and replace rear axle shafts.

20. Inspect and replace rear axle shaft seals, bearings, and retainers.

21. Measure rear axle flange runout and shaft end play; determine needed repairs.

Overview

The Classroom Manual states three purposes of the differential and axle assembly. The major components of the differential are explained and their purposes are given. Ring and pinion gear sets are dealt with in detail. Straddle mounted and overhung pinion mountings are discussed. Rear axle ratio, hunting, nonhunting, and partial nonhunting gear sets are discussed. The need for both pinion bearing and carrier bearing preload is given and preload is defined. Pinion, carrier, and axle bearings are discussed. Thrust load application for ball roller, straight roller, and tapered roller bearing axle mountings are discussed. Four types of limited-slip differential are described; cone type clutches, disc type clutches, viscous clutches, and locked differentials. Detailed operation is given for each type of limited-slip differential.

Integral and removable carrier assemblies are compared, as well as independent rear wheel suspension and differentials. Full-floating, three-quarter, and semifloating axles are described and the bearing supports used on each are illustrated. Front-wheel drive differentials and final drives are covered. The operation of drive pinion and ring final drives, and planetary gear set final drives, is described.

In the Shop Manual, diagnosis of differentials and drive axles is covered. Road test procedures, noise and vibration diagnosis, and sources of leaks are discussed. In-vehicle services such as checking the fluid level and replacing pinion seals are covered. Differential disassembly, measurement, set-up and reassembly procedures are covered in detail. Axle bearing and seal removal, inspection, and replacement procedures are also covered.

Reading Assignments

Classroom Manual, pages 155–191
Shop Manual, pages 267–331

Terms to Know

Bearing whine	Gear noise	Pinion gear
Chatter	Heel	Ramp-type differential
Chuckle	Hunting gear set	Removable carrier
Clutch pack	Integral carrier	Ring gear
Clunk	IRS	Rumble
Coast	Knocking	Semifloating axle
Companion flange	Lapping	Side gears
Cone clutch	Limited-slip differential	Straddle-mounted pinion
C-type retainer	Live axle	Swing axle
Differential case	Locked differential	Three-quarter axle
Drive	Nonhunting gear set	Toe
Drive pinion flange	Overhung-mounted pinion	Viscous coupling
Final drive	Partial nonhunting gear set	
Full-floating axle		

Lecture Outline and Notes

I. Objectives

Review the chapter's objectives.

II. Introduction

A. Describe the typical differential mounting on RWD vehicles.

B. Explain differential mounting on vehicles with independent rear suspension (IRS).

C. Describe the differential mounting on FWD vehicles.

D. Explain the basic purpose of the differential.

E. Explain the basic design of a hypoid gear set.

F. Describe the differential configuration on FWD vehicles.

G. Explain the effect differential gear ratio has on torque.

III. Function and Components

A. Explain the basic function of the differential and describe the result if differential action is not available.

B. Explain the pinion gear, ring gear, side gear, and differential pinion gear design and mounting.

IV. Differential Operation

A. Describe the flow of engine torque through the differential components.

B. Explain differential gear reduction.

C. Describe the side gear and differential pinion gear design, and explain how one drive wheel rotates faster than the opposite drive wheel while the vehicle is turning a corner.

D. Explain the differential action when one drive wheel has little or no traction on the road surface.

V. Axle Housings

A. Describe the various types of differential housings including integral carrier and removable carrier.

B. Discuss different types of differential lubricants.

VI. Differential Gears

A. Describe hypoid gear design.

B. Explain pinion and ring gear and complete differential action during hard acceleration.

C. Discuss differential and transmission gear ratios.

D. Explain final drive gear ratios.

E. Explain differential identification.

F. Describe nonhunting, partial hunting, hunting gear sets, and explain ring and pinion gear lapping.

VII. Differential Bearings

    A. Explain the purpose of various differential bearings.

    B. Describe drive pinion flange design, and explain various types of pinion gear mounting including straddle, overhung mounting.

    C. Explain the purpose of differential pinion bearing preload.

    D. Describe the differential case design.

VIII. Transaxle Final Drive Gears and Differential

    A. Describe transaxle differential design including a typical helical final drive.

    B. Describe the design of a planetary final drive in a transaxle.

    C. Explain the design of a transaxle hypoid final drive.

IX. Limited-Slip Differentials

    A. Explain the advantage of a limited-slip differential.

    B. Describe the design of a limited-slip differential including the clutch pack, cone clutches, viscous clutch, and gear-base units.

    C. Define an automatic torque biasing differential, locked differential, and gerodisc differential.

X. Drive Axle Shafts and Bearings

    A. Describe various types of drive axle shafts including live axle, full-floating axle, three-quarter or semifloating axle.

    B. Discuss various types of axle bearings including ball-type, straight-roller, and tapered-roller.

    C. Describe the drive axle design on IRS systems.

XI. Diagnosis of Differential and Drive Axles

    A. Discuss the importance of obtaining information from the customer regarding the vehicle symptoms.

    B. Explain drive, cruise, coast, and float operating conditions when road testing a vehicle to diagnose differential noise and vibration.

    C. Explain various differential noises including chuckle, knocking, clunk, gear noise, bearing rumble, bearing whine, and chatter.

    D. Discuss differential and drive shaft vibration.

    E. Describe various sources of differential lubricant leaks.

    F. Explain limited-slip differential diagnostic procedures.

XII. In-Vehicle Services

    A. Explain the procedure for checking the differential fluid level.

    B. Describe the procedure for pinion seal replacement.

XIII. Out-of-Vehicle Services

A. Discuss differential service precautions.

B. Explain the procedure for measuring differential ring gear runout.

C. Describe the preparation procedures before differential removal.

XIV. Removing Final Drive Assemblies

A. Discuss the removal and disassembly procedures for removable carrier differentials.

B. Explain the procedure for disassembling an integral carrier differential.

C. Discuss pinion gear depth and the method of adjustment.

XV. Inspection of Parts

A. Explain differential parts cleaning and inspection procedures.

XVI. Reassembling a Differential Assembly

A. Explain differential reassembling procedures including ring and pinion gear installation.

XVII. Ring and Pinion Gear Adjustments

A. Describe the use of a gauge set to measure pinion depth.

B. Explain the pinion bearing preload procedure.

C. Discuss the pinion seal replacement procedure.

D. Explain the ring gear backlash and side bearing preload measurement and adjustment procedures.

E. Describe how to obtain, interpret, and correct ring gear tooth patterns.

XVIII. Servicing FWD Final Drives

A. Explain the procedure for measuring and adjusting side gear end play in a transaxle.

B. Describe the procedure for measuring and adjusting differential bearing preload in a transaxle.

XIX. Servicing Limited-Slip Differentials

A. Describe the procedure for inspecting and assembling clutch packs, and measuring clutch pack clearance.

XX. Axle Shafts and Bearings

A. Explain removal and replacement procedures for various types of axle shafts.

B. Describe removal and replacement procedures for different types of axle bearings, including bearing and bearing bore inspection.

C. Discuss axle shaft seal replacement procedures.

D. Explain axle shaft installation procedures.

XXI. Summary

Review the material covered, emphasizing the main points and key words.

Chapter 7 Answers to Review Questions

● CLASSROOM MANUAL, PAGES 191–193

Short Answer Essays

1. Final drive is the final gear set of reduction gears in the powertrain on its way to the drive wheels.

2. A differential is needed between any two drive wheels because the two drive wheels must be at different speeds when the vehicle is turning. If the tires cannot rotate at different speeds, one will scrub on the road. This scrubbing causes abnormal tire wear.

3. Hypoid gears allow the drive shaft to be positioned low in the vehicle because the final drive pinion gear center line is below the ring gear center line. This allows the vehicle, as a whole, to be lower.

4. Three major functions of a differential are: to allow for different speeds between the two drive wheels, to multiply torque, and to change the direction of power flow.

5. The drive shaft drives the pinion gear, which is in mesh with the ring gear. The ring gear is bolted to the differential case. The power flowing from the drive pinion and ring gear causes it to rotate. The differential case normally houses the pinion gears and axle side gears, which are mounted over splines at the end of the axle shafts.

6. The difference between an integral carrier housing and a removable carrier housing is in the integral type housing: the differential carrier housing and the axle housing are the same casting, whereas in the removable type, the carrier housing can be removed from the axle housing.

7. The differences between hunting, nonhunting, and partial nonhunting gears are based on the number of teeth on the ring and pinion gears. A nonhunting gear set is one in which any one pinion gear tooth comes in contact with the same teeth on the ring gear during each revolution of the ring gear. A partial nonhunting gear set is one in which one pinion tooth comes in contact with the same teeth on the ring gear, but more than one revolution is required. The hunting gear set has all pinion gear teeth coming in contact with all of the teeth on the ring gear.

8. A viscous limited-slip differential has a viscous coupling with alternately positioned steel and friction plates connected to the two drive axles. The application of the plates relies on the resistance generated by a high-viscosity silicon fluid. When there is no rotational difference between the left- and right-side wheels, power is distributed evenly to both axles. When one wheel has less traction than the other, there is a difference in rotational speeds between the axles. This speed differential causes the silicon fluid to shear, generating viscous torque. This torque effectively reduces the difference in speed and reduces the spinning of the wheel with the least traction.

9. Limited-slip differentials are applied by torque differences between the side gears. High torque on one side gear causes the differential's pinion gears to push against the opposite side gear. The clutch is applied by this pressure, allowing power to move to that axle. A preload spring or springs assist in applying the clutch. This provides enough pressure on the clutch to drive both axles when the drive wheels have an unequal amount of traction. However, pressure of the springs is low enough to allow clutch slippage when the vehicle is turning a corner.

10. There are basically three designs by which axles are supported in a live axle: full-floating, three-quarter floating, and semifloating. These refer to where the axle bearing is placed in

relation to the axle and the housing. The bearing of a full-floating axle is located on the outside of the housing, which places all of the vehicle's weight on the axle housing with no weight on the axle. Three-quarter and semifloating axles are supported by bearings located in the housing and therefore carry some of the vehicle's weight on the axles.

Fill-in-the-Blanks

1. Pinion, ring, pinion, side
2. Integral, removable
3. Spiral, bevel gears, hypoid gears
4. Convex, concave, toe, heel
5. Pinion, ring
6. Hunting, nonhunting, partial nonhunting
7. Three, two
8. Helical, planetary, hypoid
9. Clutch pack, cone clutch, viscous clutch
10. Gerodisc

Multiple Choice

1. C
2. B
3. C
4. B
5. B
6. D
7. C
8. C
9. D
10. C

● SHOP MANUAL, PAGES 331–332

ASE-Style Review Questions

1. B
2. C
3. C
4. A
5. B
6. C
7. B
8. C
9. D
10. C

ASE Challenge Questions

1. D
2. A
3. D
4. B
5. D

Four-Wheel Drive Systems

Upon completion and review of this chapter, the student should be able to:

Classroom Manual Objectives

1. Explain the advantages and disadvantages of four-wheel drive.

2. Use the correct terminology when discussing four-wheel drive systems.

3. Describe the different designs of four-wheel drive systems and their applications.

4. Compare and contrast the components of part- and full-time four-wheel drive systems.

5. Describe the operation of various transfer case designs and their controls.

6. Identify the differences in operation and construction between manual and automatic locking front wheel hubs.

7. Identify the suspension requirements of vehicles equipped with four-wheel drive.

Shop Manual Objectives

1. Diagnose four-wheel-drive assembly noise, vibration, hard shifting, unusual steering problems, and determine needed repairs.

2. Inspect, adjust, and repair transfer case shifting mechanisms, bushings, mounts, levers, and brackets.

3. Inspect and service transfer case and components and check lube level.

4. Inspect, service, and replace front-drive shafts and Universal joints.

5. Inspect, service, and replace front-drive axle knuckles and driving shafts.

6. Inspect, service, and replace front wheel bearings and locking hubs.

7. Check four-wheel-drive unit seals.

Overview

The Classroom Manual focuses on transfer cases and related four-wheel drive systems used in passenger cars and light trucks. The differences between four-wheel drive and all-wheel drive systems are covered. The many various 4WD and AWD system designs, components, and operations are discussed in detail. Planetary gear sets are explained. Four-wheel drive suspension types are also covered.

In the Shop Manual, 4WD and AWD noise and vibration diagnosis is discussed. Inspection procedures are covered in detail. Transfer case removal, disassembly, and reassembly are also explained. Service procedures for axle housings, front axles and hubs, and wheel bearings are covered. 4WD system maintenance is also covered.

Reading Assignments

Classroom Manual, pages 195–222
Shop Manual, pages 345–379

Terms to Know

Annulus gear	King pins	Spring pads
Ball joint	Lift kits	Sprocket
Camber	Locking hubs	Sprocket carrier
Caster	On-demand 4WD	Steering damper
Center differential	Part-time 4WD	Sun gear
Chain drive	Pin-and-rocker joint	Sway bar
Driveline windup	Pitman arm	Thrust bearing races
Drive sprocket	Planetary gear set	Toe
Electromagnet clutch	Radius arm	Toe-out on turns
Full-time 4WD	Round-pin	Transfer case
Galvanic corrosion	Shock absorbers	Unsprung weight

Lecture Outline and Notes

I. Objectives

Review the chapter's objectives.

II. Introduction

A. Discuss the advantages of 4WD including how the engine's power is supplied to all four wheels.

B. Explain the disadvantages of 4WD including increased cost and weight.

III. Four-Wheel Drive Design Variations

A. Discuss how RWD vehicles are converted to 4WD.

B. Discuss how FWD vehicles are converted to 4WD.

C. Describe the construction of AWD systems with a center differential, viscous coupling, or transfer clutch to transmit power to the wheels.

D. Explain 4WD terminology.

E. Describe the typical components in a 4WD system including transfer case, drive shafts, universal joints, and front differential.

F. Discuss basic transfer case controls.

IV. 4WD Systems

A. Explain part-time 4WD systems.

B. Discuss full-time 4WD systems.

V. Transfer Cases

A. Explain the purposes of a transfer case.

B. Describe modes of transfer case operation, and explain how 4WD low range is provided in a chain-driven transfer case.

C. Describe gear-driven transfer case operation.

D. Discuss the basic operation of transfer case electrical controls.

VI. Transfer Case Designs

A. Describe a round-pin transfer case drive chain.

B. Explain planetary gear design in a transfer case.

C. Explain electronic transfer case shift control operation.

VII. Locking Hubs

A. Describe manual and automatic locking hub design and operation.

VIII. Four-Wheel Drive Suspensions

A. Describe various types of suspension systems used with 4WD systems, and explain why these suspension system designs are required with 4WD systems.

IX. Diagnosis

A. Discuss the diagnosis of various 4WD problems including bottoming out over rough terrain, swaying, front wheel shimmy, and abnormal tire wear.

B. Describe the diagnosis of noise, vibration, and shifting problems on 4WD systems.

X. Inspection

A. Explain the inspection procedures for fluid leaks, transfer case, drive shafts, suspension system components, steering system components, wheel bearings, and tires and wheels.

XI. Transfer Cases

A. Explain the proper transfer case removal procedure.

B. Describe the typical transfer case disassembly procedures.

C. Explain the typical transfer case assembly procedures.

XII. Axle Housings and Differentials

A. Describe drive shaft service procedures.

B. Explain the proper removal and installation procedures for manual and automatic locking hubs.

C. Describe the removal and installation procedures for front drive axles.

XIII. Wheel Bearings

A. Discuss front wheel bearing adjustment procedures.

XIV. Typical 4WD Modifications

A. Discuss the typical modifications that are attempted on 4WD systems, and explain the effect of these modifications.

XV. Maintenance

A. **Explain 4WD system maintenance, and discuss the results of inadequate maintenance.**

XVI. Summary

Review the material covered, emphasizing the main points and key words.

Chapter 8 Answers to Review Questions

● CLASSROOM MANUAL, PAGES 223–225

Short Answer Essays

1. The main advantage of a four-wheel drive vehicle over a two-wheel drive vehicle is improved traction and handling.
2. The main differences between four-wheel drive and all-wheel drive is that four-wheel drive uses a separate transfer case and allows the driver to select the transferring of the engine's power to two or four wheels. All-wheel drives do not use a transfer case; instead, they use a center differential to transmit engine power to the front and rear axles. This system will not allow the driver to select between two- and four-wheel drive.
3. The transfer case receives the engine's power from the transmission and transfers it to the drive shafts leading to the front and rear drive axles.
4. When the front locking hubs are locked to the front axles, four-wheel drive results; when they are unlocked, the front wheels are free to rotate at different speeds.
5. The differences between an integrated 4WD system and an "on-demand" 4WD system is that the integrated system uses either a computer or a clutch to adjust the torque split to the drive axles depending on which wheels have traction, while the on-demand system provides power to the second axle only when 4WD is selected by the driver.
6. A part-time 4WD system can be shifted from 2WD to 4WD. A full-time 4WD system is always in 4WD.
7. The three main components that are added to a 2WD system to make it 4WD are a transfer case, front drive shaft, and front differential.
8. The purpose of an interaxle is to allow the rear and front wheels to turn at different speeds.
9. Chain drives are used in many transfer cases because they reduce weight, are efficient and quiet, and allow for drive gear placement flexibility.
10. A planetary gear set is made up of three major components: the sun gear, which is usually splined to the input shaft; the planetary gear assembly, which is comprised of the planet gears and carrier and is attached to the output shaft; and the ring gear. By holding or releasing the ring gear, gear reduction can be achieved through the sun gear driving the planetary gears and carrier.

Fill-in-the-Blanks

1. Four, two; four, four
2. Sun, pinion, planetary carrier, ring
3. Ring
4. Driveline wind-up
5. Independent front
6. Vacuum, electric, linkage

7. Two-wheel drive high, four-wheel drive high, neutral, four-wheel drive low
8. Differential
9. Locking hubs
10. Differential, drive shafts

Multiple Choice

1. C
2. C
3. B
4. C
5. A
6. C
7. C
8. B
9. A
10. C

● SHOP MANUAL, PAGES 380–381

ASE-Style Review Questions

1. B
2. C
3. B
4. C
5. A
6. C
7. C
8. C
9. B
10. B

ASE Challenge Questions

1. B
2. C
3. A
4. C
5. D

Advanced Four-Wheel Drive Systems

Upon completion and review of this chapter, the student should be able to:

Classroom Manual Objectives

1. Use the correct terminology when discussing 4WD systems.

2. Describe the different designs of 4WD systems and their applications.

3. Compare and contrast the components of part- and full-time 4WD systems.

4. Discuss the purpose of an interaxle differential and the design variations used by the industry.

5. Discuss the purpose, operation, and application of a viscous coupling in 4WD systems.

6. Explain the operation of some common AWD systems.

Shop Manual Objectives

1. Explain the basic procedures for diagnosing shift problems on 4WD systems.

2. Test, service, and replace center differential assemblies.

3. Test and replace viscous coupling units.

4. Diagnose vacuum operated "shift-on-the-fly" systems.

5. Diagnose on-demand 4WD systems.

6. Diagnose AWD systems.

7. Diagnose differential lock systems.

Overview

The Classroom Manual deals with four-wheel drive system designs. Proper terminology is covered. The use of common terms and industry standard terms are compared. Designs of various systems, their components, controls, and operating modes are discussed.

All wheel drive (AWD) systems are also covered. Their major components, including interaxle differentials and viscous couplings, are explained in detail. Several specific manufacturers' systems are described.

The Shop Manual covers system diagnosis, service, and repair. Inspection and diagnosis of system controls are discussed. Interaxle differential and viscous clutch diagnosis and service are covered. System diagnosis and component testing and replacement on "shift-on-the-fly," on-demand, and AWD systems are discussed in depth. Scan tool diagnosis is also covered.

Reading Assignments

Classroom Manual, pages 227–243
Shop Manual, pages 393–415

Terms to Know

Data link connector (DLC)	Duty cycle	Shift mode sleeve
Diagnostic trouble code (DTC)	Duty solenoid	Silicone oil
	Power transfer unit (PTU)	Viscous coupling

Lecture Outline and Notes

I. Objectives

Review the chapter objectives.

II. Introduction

A. Describe 4WD systems based on RWD and FWD configurations.

B. Describe full-time and part-time 4WD systems.

C. Explain why limited-slip differentials are used with some 4WD systems.

D. Describe the locking action of a center differential.

E. Explain automatic 4WD systems that use a computer-controlled clutch in the transfer case to control the torque split between the front and rear axles.

III. Operational Modes

A. Explain the 4WD automatic mode that provides power to the front and rear wheels as required.

B. Describe the 4WD high mode that provides full power to both axles.

C. Explain the 4WD low mode that provides full power to both axles with a lower gear ratio.

IV. All-Wheel Drive Systems

A. Explain the basic design, operation, and advantages of AWD systems.

B. Explain the operation of AWD systems with a single speed transfer case in the transaxle.

C. Describe the operation of AWD systems with an interaxle.

D. Describe the operation of integrated AWD systems with an integrated transaxle and transfer case.

E. Explain the operation of on-demand AWD systems, including the wheel speed sensors, multiple disc clutch, and duty solenoid.

F. Explain the basic purpose and operation of a viscous coupling.

G. Describe the basic operation of a center differential.

H. Explain the basic operation of an electronically-controlled AWD system.

V. Viscous Couplings

A. Explain the basic applications and purpose of a viscous coupling.

B. Describe the operation of a viscous coupling.

C. Describe the advantages of a viscous coupling.

D. Explain the design and operation of a Haldex clutch.

E. Describe the basic design, purpose, and advantage of a Quaife differential.

VI. Newer 4WD Design Variations

    A. Describe the basic design and operation of Acura and Honda VTM-4 system.

    B. Explain the basic design and operation of Chrysler AWD systems.

    C. Describe the basic design and operation of Ford Trac II systems.

    D. Discuss the basic design and operation of Hyundai On-Demand systems.

    E. Explain the basic design and operation of the Subaru VTD system.

VII. General Shift Control

    A. Discuss inspection procedures for 4WD and AWD systems.

    B. Explain the basic diagnosis of electrical/electronic 4WD and AWD systems.

    C. Describe the basic diagnosis of vacuum and linkage problems on 4WD and AWD.

VIII. Center Differentials

    A. Describe the typical service procedures for center differentials.

IX. Viscous Couplings

    A. Describe typical diagnostic procedures for viscous couplings.

X. Shift-on-the-Fly Systems

    A. Explain shift-on-the-fly system indicator lamp diagnosis.

    B. Explain shift-on-the-fly vacuum system diagnosis.

    C. Discuss scan tool diagnosis of shift-on-the-fly systems.

    D. Describe individual testing of shift-on-the-fly system components.

XI. AWD Systems

    A. Explain basic AWD system diagnosis.

XII. Differential Lock Systems

    A. Explain differential lock system warning lamp diagnosis.

    B. Describe rear differential diagnostic procedures.

    C. Explain center differential diagnostic procedures.

XIII. Active Height Control Suspension (AHC)

    A. Discuss active height control problems.

XIV. Summary

Review the material covered, emphasizing the main points and key words.

Chapter 9 Answers to Review Questions

● CLASSROOM MANUAL, PAGES 243–245

Short Answer Essays

1. A viscous coupling works by using fluid to transfer torque from one set of plates that are attached to the input shaft, to another set of plates attached to the output. It is used in AWD systems to improve the mobility factor under difficult driving conditions.

2. A 4WD system needs to be engaged by the driver, whereas an AWD system constantly provides power to all four wheels.

3. Larger 4WD trucks and SUVs are typically based on RWD vehicles, whereas smaller 4WD trucks and SUVs are normally based on FWD vehicles.

4. Low range is designed to provide extra power in off-road situations such as sand or steep grades.

5. The most commonly used limited-slip units in a center differential are a viscous clutch, cone clutch, and multiple-plate clutch assembly.

6. AWD systems automatically react to normal or slippery road conditions without driver interaction.

7. A viscous coupling is basically a drum containing thick silicone fluid that houses several closely fitted steel discs. One set of plates is connected to the front wheels and the other to the rear. When the plates spin, the fluid gets hot, thickens, and acts as a connector between the input and output plates.

8. The purpose of an interaxle differential is to prevent driveline windup.

9. The most complex AWD system ever developed was used on the Porsche 959, which did not wait for wheel slip before transferring torque. The system monitored the vehicle's steering angle, lateral acceleration, throttle position, yaw rate, and wheel spin. It attempted to transfer torque where needed before it was absolutely necessary.

10. The Haldex unit is much like a hydraulic pump in which the housing and a piston are connected to one shaft and a piston actuator connected to the other. When a front wheel slips, the input shaft to the Haldex unit spins faster then its output shaft. This causes the pump to immediately generate oil flow. The oil flow and pressure engages the multi-disc clutch to send power to the rear wheels. This happens extremely quickly because an electric pump and accumulator keep the circuit primed. The oil from the pump flows to the clutch's piston to compress the clutch pack. The oil returns to the reservoir through a controllable valve, which adjusts the oil pressure and the force on the clutch pack. An electronic control module controls the valve and also determines when to decouple the axles to prevent the rear brakes from braking the front axle. In high slip conditions, high pressure is delivered to the clutch pack. In tight curves or at high speeds, a much lower pressure is provided. When there is no difference in speed between the front and rear axles, the pump does not supply pressure to the clutch pack.

Fill-in-the-Blanks

1. Transfer case, center differential, viscous clutch
2. Speed sensitive
3. Gear-operated
4. Driveline windup
5. Interaxle
6. Viscosity; shearing; volumetric
7. Shear

8. Viscous control
9. Least; most
10. Locking, viscous

Multiple Choice

1. C
2. C
3. A
4. C
5. B
6. C
7. C
8. A
9. A
10. D

● SHOP MANUAL, PAGES 416–417

ASE-Style Review Questions

1. B
2. C
3. B
4. C
5. C
6. C
7. A
8. C
9. C
10. C

ASE Challenge Questions

1. C
2. D
3. C
4. D
5. C

Drivetrain Electrical and Electronic Systems

CHAPTER

10

Upon completion and review of this chapter, the student should be able to:

Classroom Manual Objectives

1. Understand and explain the basic principles of electricity.

2. Understand and explain the basic difference between electricity and electronics.

3. Understand and define the terms voltage, current, and resistance.

4. Name the various electrical components and their uses in electrical circuits.

5. Understand and describe the purpose and operation of a clutch safety switch.

6. Understand and describe the purpose and operation of a reverse lamp switch.

7. Understand and describe the purpose and operation of an upshift light and a high gear switch.

8. Understand and describe the location and operation of ABS speed sensor circuits.

9. Understand and describe the purpose and operation of a shift blocking circuit.

Shop Manual Objectives

1. Diagnose electrical problems by logic and symptom description.

2. Perform troubleshooting procedures using meters, test lights, and jumper wires.

3. Repair electrical wiring.

4. Replace electrical connectors.

5. Locate, test, adjust, and replace electrical switches on a transmission.

6. Locate, test, and replace transmission-related electrical solenoids.

7. Test and replace electromagnetic clutches.

8. Diagnose transmission-related electronic control circuits.

Overview

The Classroom Manual includes a discussion of basic electricity/electronics and the electrical and electronic circuits related to the manual transmission/transaxle. It covers those components affected by the vehicle electrical systems and the connection between vehicle electronics and the manual transmission.

In the Shop Manual, electrical system servicing, as it pertains to manual transmissions, is covered. Electrical diagnosis, testing, and repair are discussed. Servicing of electrical components is also covered. Vehicle electronics are introduced.

Reading Assignments

Classroom Manual, pages 247–274
Shop Manual, pages 433–463

Terms to Know

Actuator

Alternating current

American wire gauge (AWG)

Ammeter

Ampere

Analog

Backup light switch

Chassis ground

Circuit breaker

Clutch safety switch

Conductors

Controllers

Current

Digital

Diode

Direct current

Digital multimeter (DMM)

Digital volt/ohmmeter (DVOM)

Electricity

Electromotive force (EMF)

Field of flux

Fusible link

Impedance

Insulators

Integrated circuit

Load

Loads

Maxi-fuse

Multimeter

Ohm

Ohmmeter

Ohm's law

Open

Output driver

Potentiometers

Programmable read-only memory (PROM)

Random access memory (RAM)

Reference voltage (V_{ref}) sensors

Relay

Resistance

Rheostats

Scan tool

Schematic

Self-shifting manual transmission

Semiconductor

Short

Solenoids

Test light

Transistor

Voltage

Voltage drop

Voltage generating devices

Voltmeter

Volts

Lecture Outline and Notes

I. Objectives

Review the chapter's objectives.

II. Introduction

A. **Discuss applications of electricity/electronics in manual drive trains.**

B. **Explain the importance of understanding electricity/electronics.**

C. **Discuss the importance of proper terminology in automotive electricity/electronics.**

D. **Explain the importance of understanding electricity/electronics as it relates to accurate diagnosis of automotive electrical/electronic systems.**

III. Basic Electricity

A. **Discuss atomic structure including electrons, protons, and neutrons.**

B. **Explain electron movement and current flow.**

C. **Describe the two sources of electricity on a vehicle.**

D. **Explain the measurement of electricity including volts, amperes, and ohms.**

E. Define current flow, resistance, and electrical pressure.

F. Explain basic electrical circuits, and explain how current flow is controlled in a circuit.

G. Explain Ohm's law formula and discuss how this formula is used when diagnosing automotive electrical circuits.

H. Explain electrical circuit components including power sources, conductors, loads, controllers, and protection devices.

I. Explain electrical circuit components including types of resistors, variable resistors (rheostats), potentiometers, thermistors, switches, relays, and solenoids. Describe typical automotive electrical circuits and where these components are located.

J. Describe electromagnestism and give examples of the application of electromagnet principles in automotive electrical/electronic systems.

K. Explain induced voltage and describe how the amount of induced voltage is controlled.

L. Define electrical conductors and insulators.

IV. Basics of Electronics

A. Define semiconductors, and describe several types of semiconductor devices including diodes, transistors, and integrated circuits.

B. Explain basic sensor purpose, and describe reference voltage sensors.

C. Explain sensors that are voltage generating devices.

D. Describe communication signals.

E. Explain and provide examples of actuators in automotive electronic systems.

V. Clutch Safety Switch

A. Explain the purpose, circuit connection, and operation of a clutch safety switch.

VI. Reverse Lamp Switch

A. Describe the purpose, circuit connection, and operation of a reverse lamp switch.

VII. High Gear Switch

A. Explain the purpose, circuit connection, and operation of a high gear switch.

VIII. Upshift Lamp Circuit

A. Describe the purpose, circuit connection, and operation of an upshift lamp circuit.

IX. ABS Speed Sensor Circuits

A. Describe ABS sensor signals and explain how they are used in automotive electronic systems.

X. Shift Blocking

A. Explain the operation of shift blocking switches.

XI. Electrical Clutches

A. Describe the design and operation of electrical clutches.

B. Explain the basic operation of a self-shifting manual transmission.

XII. Other Electronic Systems

A. Describe other electronic systems used in drive train applications.

XIII. Basic Electrical Diagnosis

A. Discuss basic electrical diagnosis including electrical circuits, loads or resistance, and chassis grounds.

B. Explain electrical wiring diagrams and interpret wiring diagram symbols.

C. Describe electrical problems including open, short, and short to ground.

D. Explain basic automotive electrical test equipment including voltmeters, ammeters, and ohmmeters, multimeters, test lights, and jumper wires.

XIV. General Guidelines

A. Explain general guidelines for basic electrical circuit diagnosis including the diagnosis of shorted, open, and grounded circuits.

XV. Basic Electrical Repairs

A. Describe basic electrical circuit repair and diagnosis including connector installation, fuse and fusible link diagnosis, maxi-fuse diagnosis, and circuit breaker diagnosis.

XVI. Switches

A. Explain typical switch diagnosis and adjustment using examples such as the clutch safety switch and backup light switch.

XVII. Speed Sensors

A. Describe wheel speed sensor inspection, diagnosis, and adjustment.

XVIII. Solenoids

A. Discuss solenoid inspection and diagnosis.

XIX. Electromagnetic Clutches

A. Explain electromagnetic clutch diagnosis.

XX. Electronic Circuits

    A. Explain scan tool and trouble code diagnosis of electronic circuits.

    B. Discuss self-shifting transmissions.

    C. Explain shift light operation.

    D. Describe electronic shift blocking circuit diagnosis.

XXI. Summary

Review the material covered, emphasizing the main points and key words.

Chapter 10 Answers to Review Questions

● CLASSROOM MANUAL, PAGES 274–276

Short Answer Essays

1. An automobile relies on the vehicle's battery and the alternator (charging system) for a source of electrical power.
2. In order to maintain a flow of electricity, there must be voltage and resistance, as well as a complete circuit.
3. Electricity is the controlled movement of electrons.
4. Voltage is electrical pressure and current is the movement or flow of electricity.
5. There must be an electrical source of power, a load, a conductor to the load from the power source, and a conductor from the load back to the power source.
6. Ohm's law states that it takes one volt of electrical pressure to push one amp of electrical current through one ohm of resistance.
7. A rheostat is a variable resistor that controls voltage by changing the current in the circuit. A potentiometer is a variable resistor that controls voltage by dividing the voltage in the circuit.
8. A fixed resistor has a resistance value that remains nearly constant. A variable resistor can have its values changed by an operator, a condition, or a mechanical device.
9. There are two basic types of sensors used in an automotive computer system: reference voltage sensors and voltage generating sensors. Reference voltage sensors send a varying signal to the computer based on a reference voltage supplied by the computer. Voltage generating sensors send varying voltage signals to the computer that are generated by the sensor itself.
10. Shift blocking is a feature designed to prevent the driver from shifting from first gear to second or third gear under certain driving conditions based on engine temperature, vehicle speed, and throttle opening. It is used to ensure good fuel economy.

Fill-in-the-Blanks

1. Chemical reaction, electromagnetism
2. Amperes, volts, ohms
3. Transmission, shifter
4. Fuses, maxi-fuses, fuse links, circuit breakers
5. Switches
6. Nucleus
7. Ohms

8. Semiconductor
9. Analog, digital
10. Drive axle assembly, ring gear

Multiple Choice

1. C
2. C
3. D
4. B
5. C
6. C
7. C
8. C
9. C
10. C

● SHOP MANUAL, PAGES 464–465

ASE-Style Review Questions

1. C
2. B
3. C
4. C
5. D
6. C
7. C
8. C
9. D
10. D

ASE Challenge Questions

1. B
2. C
3. A
4. A
5. B

Answers to the ASE Practice Examination (Shop Manual) (Pages 479–483)

1. A	11. B	21. B	31. B	41. A
2. D	12. C	22. C	32. B	42. D
3. C	13. D	23. C	33. C	43. B
4. A	14. C	24. D	34. D	44. D
5. D	15. C	25. A	35. A	45. A
6. A	16. A	26. A	36. A	46. C
7. B	17. D	27. D	37. B	47. A
8. A	18. D	28. C	38. A	48. C
9. B	19. A	29. B	39. B	49. A
10. C	20. C	30. C	40. A	50. C